An Analyst in Training

An Analyst in Training

Psychoanalytic Candidacy Amid COVID and Other Distractions

Graeme Daniels

BLOOMSBURY ACADEMIC
NEW YORK • LONDON • OXFORD • NEW DELHI • SYDNEY

BLOOMSBURY ACADEMIC
Bloomsbury Publishing Inc
1359 Broadway, New York, NY 10018, USA
50 Bedford Square, London, WC1B 3DP, UK
29 Earlsfort Terrace, Dublin 2, Ireland

First published in the United States of America 2025

Cover design: Dustin Watson
Cover art by Don Mathews

Library of Congress Cataloguing-in-Publication Data Available

ISBN: HB: 979-8-8818-0640-8
PB: 979-8-8818-0641-5
ePDF: 979-8-7651-5419-9
eBook: 979-8-8818-0642-2

Typeset by Deanta Global Publishing Services, Chennai, India

For Jason & Judy

Contents

Foreword

In 1938, when forced to leave Austria, then under Nazi rule, and after the arrest and interrogation of his daughter Anna, Freud was forced to sign a document for the Gestapo stating that he had not suffered mistreatment. After signing it, he notoriously added in his own handwriting: "I can strongly recommend the Gestapo to everyone." Initially, his biographer Peter Gay interpreted this humorous observation as an unconscious suicide attempt, given that the boldness of the comment could've put Freud's life at risk if Nazi authorities had realized his subtle irony. Later, however, Gay was able to recognize in this attitude not only Freud's great courage and vitality but also his irrepressible sense of humor.

In a similar manner, this book coming to fruition is an amusing, if not an utterly tragic, realization. I say that not only because its object—psychoanalytic training—is a very serious matter and we—Graeme and myself—are advocates for taking it seriously, but mainly because we advocate for it also being the subject of mockery. But why mock psychoanalytic training? Well, because it elicits such strictness and even rigidness, sacrifice and abstinence, that we believe ridding ourselves of some of that strictness may be wise—something maybe not that different from what Freud was doing with the Gestapo. And, yes, I'm comparing institutional psychoanalysis to the Nazi secret police. Two paragraphs in and I'm already blaspheming.

But let's put this on Graeme: How does he dare? Writing something like this? Psychoanalysis is serious and complex, and very much rightly so. It is a craft too oblique to be considered rigorously scientific or medical, too concerned with the patient's suffering to be free like art or philosophy. It stands equidistant from so many fields of knowledge and different clinical practices that it receives criticism from all of them. And even while struggling to be a cohesive, integrated, and ultimately useful method with which to approach and treat emotional suffering, we expect a lot from it. "We" being the public, other informed technicians such as researchers and other licensed psychotherapists, but specially psychoanalysts themselves. So, you see, psychoanalysis equips its practitioners with a training that is long and as thorough as it is arduous, but in a way also lays them bare and unprotected—and necessarily so. We take long to get somewhere, and it's frequently an uncertain place. It is a delicate and humbling task, and in the end we tend to integrate a sort of conviction that it is valid, solid, and still the best approach there is. Because it is.

So why mock it? Well, I believe that in all its seriousness, its importance and responsibility, few seem to be brave enough to use humor while practicing it, writing about it, let alone taking the piss at it publicly. Unless, of course, you're trying to prove it being wrong. But if you're deeply invested in psychoanalysis, as Graeme and I are, you don't see that happening much.

When I first met Graeme in 2019, in the first few days under the context of a visiting study program to the San Francisco Center for Psychoanalysis, I was feeling very jet-lagged and like a somewhat intimidated, out-of-place foreign body. And I was feeling this even as I was in a deeply privileged position of having a lot of attention, affection, and curiosity directed toward me. Everyone was being very nice, from the institute's faculty members to my hosts, themselves analysts. In fact, pretty much everyone I encountered from the psychoanalytic community was like that. However, while meeting different analysts and fellow psychoanalytic candidates was my main purpose when I got into the program, I was longing for and missing something, even if this was not immediately clear to me. I now think I needed to feel anchored there, something I was missing in my training at home, albeit in a different way.

My experience of psychoanalytic training was very enriching, if sometimes daunting. I came from its seminar segment with a lot of knowledge piled up but also a lot of questions about how I could attain that holy grail that is the "psychoanalytical identity." Graeme made me feel that he too was having a similar experience. We got acquainted at an event where he was presenting a case and where I began to appreciate for the first time his approach to clinical work and clinic thinking. I particularly enjoyed his way of presenting, with a literary British accent and sardonic undertone emphasizing a very subtle and restrained sense of humor that went unnoticed to a large part of the audience present, the kind of humor that allows you to appreciate not only the quality of the relationship and work going on but also the kind of therapist Graeme is: present, permeable, even holding, but definitely not there to mother you. He could sometimes be abrupt, though never brash. It seemed to me that he wanted the patient in the case he was describing—an older, tough man with some addiction-derived issues, old enough to be his father—to feel him present but not to get too comfortable. I remembered thinking that the patient had to be on his toes in that period of the treatment, that he had to respect Graeme or could very easily lose interest in the work—or worse, in his therapist. Graeme was showing us just how he was performing that task. I think to this day that doing this is something you don't learn in psychoanalytic seminars. And Graeme was doing it in a subtle way and with this very, very implicit, almost unnoticeable, dark humor that was keeping the patient engaged with him, and me engaged with Graeme, who ended up also giving me the anchorage I needed. He gave me that because he was able to use humor in a way that made me connect not only with him but also with myself again. I felt kinship. And my headache disappeared.

We went on to become friends. Close ones. Friends who visit, even if living more than nine thousand miles away from each other. Friends who change and challenge how one another lives and faces life. But we always do it with psychoanalysis close by.

One of our ongoing subjects of discussion for years now is psychoanalytic practice and training. We joke about it, mainly its strict rules and shortcomings, it being less than ideal (how could it be different?), all the while recognizing its main premises and objectives. And there are times where it's just too hard to resist not driving psychoanalytic thought against itself (i.e., its representatives) or using plain common sense to question it. Graeme and I took a liking to doing that, like two hardcore football (soccer) fans complaining about their club manager's decisions while at the same time being able to viciously murder anyone who would dare to say something vaguely derogatory about our colors. It could be as childish as that. But we also took a liking to being serious with our humor because we could see that it enabled us to deconstruct some very intricate concepts without necessarily watering them down. The very notion of intellectual dilution of complex concepts has always seemed threatening to psychoanalysis, ever since Freud. Which equally says volumes about its intrinsic conceptual frailty. But why does this happen? I mean, why does using humor against psychoanalysis seem so wrong? I dare to say that there may be a metapsychological reason behind it. And again, it might have something to do with the institution and its representatives (i.e., our institutional Superegos).

We were always very aware of the Trojan horse fallacy, as if we were being traitors to the cause. Throughout its history, psychoanalysis has always had a lot of enemies, people who would position themselves so intensely against it that it's just undeniable that Freud got something right. Nevertheless, our beefs were most times not so much against psychoanalytic theory or clinical practice itself as they were against training and institutions. A kind of institutionalized Manichaeism, or maybe something inherent to organizations or groups of people. Nevertheless, we need institutions, and we very much value and respect them and ultimately desire to see them working better.

But what is that about metapsychology and mocking psychoanalytic training?

A Brief Theoretical Framework for Taking the Piss: Going Against and Aligning With the Superego

While doing research on the relationship between humor and depression, Pinheiro (2011) wrote a literature revision that I felt to be very helpful. She mentions that, even though humor is usually looked at from the perspective of a defense mechanism and at the service of pathology (Coimbra de Matos, 2011), it can also be a way to articulate feelings like shame and guilt. And we can see that connection more clearly when we have as a main determinant the presence and influence of the Superego.

The Superego was first properly introduced by Freud in 1923, and even though it is no longer mentioned in psychoanalytic discourse as it was before, Pinheiro sees it as a pivotal concept, analogous to the discovery of the Cartesian theory or the existence of God, "emerging as a unifying response to issues arising from incongruent clinical observations, such as the need for punishment or negative therapeutic reactions (Donnet, 2005). In Freud's psychoanalytic project, it is one of the structural concepts of metapsychology, consistently based on an almost fictional logic (Laplanche & Pontalis, 1967) and a transcendent language (Lansky, 2004)" (Pinheiro, 2011, p. 3).

But why is this theorization about the Superego useful for us? It's as useful as metapsychology itself: as we understand the way it works, we get access to an approach to psychological phenomena that in a first glance just seems dissonant. For instance, if aggressive functioning helps us understand phenomena such as guilt, shame, and even depression, will it help us look at the supposedly "positive" psychological dimensions such as the sense of humor? Maybe it can also help us better understand Graeme's enterprise.

Pinheiro believes that even though the Superego was revised throughout the last century and a half, especially after Melanie Klein's fundamental contributions, the vision of it as an instance of the mind with a predominantly severe and aggressive functioning remains. As Chabert (2007) underlines, it's a rare thing to find references to the Superego as benevolent or even protective. Pinheiro follows Chabert, suggesting that

> this often-neglected component is explained by the "peace" that the renunciation of transgressions makes possible for the Self, as well as by the possibility of the Self being narcissistically nourished by the Superego when in a peaceful relationship with (that inner) authority. What Chabert seems to emphasize is that benevolence and permissiveness have nothing to do with dismissal: protection does not signal an anarchic freedom but an internalization

> of interdicts and prohibitions. Superego-derived integration thus becomes a condition for that "peacefulness," translating into an internal enrichment and an expansion of the limits of the Self. . . . Thus, we are faced with an instance that more adequately portrays the "inner father" (Newirth, 2006), in the sense of law and model, in its two dimensions: that of attack and frustration, that of protection and purpose. (Pinheiro, 2011, p. 4)

In other words, an internal containing father, able to make you laugh and sometimes protect you from some of life's harshness and maybe even yourself. Pinheiro goes on saying that humor brings out

> the capacity to understand the importance of laughing at the expense of your own self and of your place in the world. Humor that does not imply pleasure in suffering but in fact helps oneself reflect and take a look at oneself and one's limits despite the pain. . . . Making humor reveals a mature capacity to recognize internal conflict and accept oneself, even when this knowledge goes beyond narcissistic limitations. This humor . . . requires the assumption of a modesty that is sustained by the strength of the Self and simultaneously requires recognition and consideration of the other. (pp. 6–7)

This way, we look at humor not only as a coping mechanism but also as a way to view the world and integrate it. From a mental economical perspective, humor is a way of obtaining pleasure despite the presence of unpleasant affects or emotions, integrating those suffering-causing affects in the self. It enables an articulation between the pleasure principle and the reality principle and, through this, creates a system that synthesizes the primary and the secondary process.

Kohut (1966) saw humor as a possibility of integrating affect and suffering. He associates the concept with a mature transformation of narcissism and, referring to death anxiety, highlights that the sense of humor allows a confrontation with death that does not imply the denial of reality. Another author, Bergeret (1973), suggests that humor preserves representations linked to distressing affect, enabling a kind of "humor work" that makes use of different mechanisms of the primary process to which secondary elaboration is associated. It is this work that allows us to view humor as an outline of the elaboration (and integration) of different kinds of anxieties through the creation of new connections and different modes of discharge in relation to the object.

Thus, more than a defense mechanism against negative affect, humor seems to be a work of psychic elaboration, allowing the integration of suffering and distressing reality, bringing humor closer to sublimation. This mechanism of integration and the transformation of reality that humor seems to provide suggests comparing the sense of humor to creativity, to the elaboration and creation of something new, a new thought. In this sense, one can think of an approach to Bion's alpha function, where the unthinkable becomes thinkable (cf. Grotstein, 1999). For Coimbra de Matos (2011), "The secret or art of a sense of humor lies in the discrepant associative link between real and invented meaning. . . . The hilarious effect is placed more . . . in the associative link than in the new meaning found; it results from the process that builds meaning" (p. 251). This statement suggests the possibility of someone smiling with the creation of a possible idea in the mind, less saturated with anxiety or at least distanced enough from that which causes anxiety. That also underlines the importance of language and symbolization in the device of humor.

In short, more than a process of escaping from reality and affection, humor is a way to elaborate. Its pleasure-obtaining feature is derived not from the denial of reality (internal and external) nor from suffering. The triumph of the "humorist" is the possibility of articulating the representation of the tragedy and the creation of a new meaning, without abandoning the test of reality. Pleasure is thus possible despite negative affect and unpleasant reality and has a particular purpose: reinforcing the self.

This is not to be confused with narcissistic grandiosity. Kohut (1966) goes on to endorse the idea against humor as psychopathological when he distinguishes the "authentic sense of humor" from "play" or "irony," those being expressions of narcissistic vulnerability. That vulnerability would prove to be an insufficient elaboration, just the same phenomenon "under a new disguise" (Kohut, 1966, p. 267). The "authentic sense of humor" would imply a recognition of the narcissistic limitations, besides an internal tolerance of the self's fragilities, far from the needs for grandiose affirmations of perfection.

Getting back to Freud, the "superiority" of the sense of humor results from an identification with authority (father) that allows the threats of reality to be treated as "jokes." A bit like a "subject who treats himself like a child and simultaneously plays the role of superior adult towards this child" (Freud, 1927/1994, p. 138)—which helps us better understand the appearance of Holden Caulfield as a recurrent voice in this book. To explain this curious alternation of positions in the psyche, Freud adds that humor underlines an investment by the Superego, allowing the self to bound the possibilities of suffering: "the Superego, in humor, speaks to an intimidated Self, comforting him with love" (p. 140). Through this, we're seeing that the Superego does not, as in melancholia, exclusively oppress the self but may also rather push away reality, use illusion to console and free the self from suffering.

Ultimately, humor seems above all else to allow thinking about the integration of failure and the liberation from suspicions of infraction—even though we do feel we transgressed our teachings every time we fall outside of orthodoxy, outside *the right way*, outside *the standard*—without falling into narcissistic omnipotence or the aggression of the object, mainly because in humor we see a differentiation between the Superego (normative or ideal) and the self.

I believe this book stems from the need to be able to do all of this. Without much of a protective psychoanalytic father, Graeme and I leaned on each other, making fun of training, as brothers do. We rebelled like adolescents against our beloved yet strict parents, against the ones who transmit the canonical scrolls. And we tried to do this while remaining ourselves, those selves that we're sent to find and understand (and be understood) through analysis, training, and work with patients. We also did that by using humor and friendship, needing solace and support to face some of its harshness, protective solidarity against a severe recruitment. What better way?

References

Bergeret, J. (1973). Pour une métapsychologie de l'humour. *Revue Française de Psychanalyse, 37*(4), 539–565.

Chabert, C. (2007). La malaise dans la culture et la question du surmoi. *Canadian Journal of Psychoanalysis, 15*, 215–237.

Coimbra de Matos, A. (2011). O humor segundo a psicopatologia. In *Relação de qualidade: penso em ti* (pp. 239–254). Climepsi.

Donnet, J.-L. (2005). Surmoi. In A. Mijolla, B. Golse, S. Mijolla-Mellor & R. Perron (Eds.), *Dictionnaire international de la psychanalyse* (pp. 1754–1756). Hachette Littératures.

Freud, S. (1994). L'humour. In J. Laplanche (Series Ed.), Bourguignon & Cotet (Vol. Eds.), *Ouvres completes: Vol. XVIII, 1926–1930* (pp. 135–140) (R. Lainé & J. Stute-Cadiot, Trans.). Presses Universitaires de France. (Original work published in 1927.)

Grotstein, J. S. (1999). Humor and its relation to the unconscious. In J. Barron (Ed.), *Humor and psyche: Psychoanalytic perspectives* (pp. 69–86). Analytic Press.

Kohut, H. (1966). *Análise do self.* Imago Editora.

Lansky, M. (2004). Conscience and the project of a psychoanalytic science of human nature: Clarification of the usefulness of the superego concept. *Psychoanalytic Inquiry, 24*(2), 151–174.

Laplanche, J., & Pontalis, J.-B. (1967). *Vocabulaire de la psychanalyse*. Presses Universitaires de France.

Newirth, J. (2006). Jokes and their relation to the unconscious: Humor as a fundamental emotional experience. *Psychoanalytic Dialogues, 16*(5), 557–571.

Pinheiro, M. T. C. (2011). *Um estudo exploratório sobre o sentido de humor e as suas relações com a culpa, a vergonha e a depressão* [master's thesis]. Universidade de Lisboa.

Acknowledgments

I'd like to thank the following people for their influence and support: Lara Weyland, for encouraging me to move to the dark side, as she once put it; Elizabeth Stuart and Eric Miller, for being a welcoming and good-humored presence throughout. I'd like to thank the members of my cohort and all the candidate members who waded through training with me during the years 2019 to 2023. I'd like to thank my supervisors, Sam Chase, Robin Deutsch, and Chuck Fisher, for their learned instruction and patience, and the leadership, administrative staff, and faculty of SFCP for their diligence and ongoing dedication to psychoanalysis. I'd also like to thank my analyst. A special thanks goes to Pedro Job, a fellow candidate, invaluable consultant for this book, and a best friend during a difficult time. Lastly, I'd like to thank, as ever, my beloved wife, Maria.

III.

Introduction
Desire, Wanting More

I'd heard it again only recently, the question: What made you want to become a psychoanalyst? I was struck by its past-tense quality, its trite formality. It may have felt like a trick question because my true reasons for pursuing this career path are unconscious. That's what the person will have thought too, and when you're in training you concern yourself with what others think. I won't have thought this originally, when I was training to be a psychotherapist years ago, though to be fair, then-mentor or supervisor types will have asked similar interview-like queries. They seemed ordinarily interested in my goals, not suggesting that I'd be unaware of my true needs as they had been, as perhaps most mental health professionals are. This latter-day question feels leading, as if becoming a psychoanalyst is a foregone conclusion for those who start down that path. How presumptuous. How supportive, I may have once thought. I travel back to 2018, a year of being impressed by my voice, as I then knew it. I was contemplating full psychoanalytic training, feeling ready for the last major training of my professional life. Better make it a good one, I thought. Better yet, better go for the most challenging, most expensive, most time-consuming, life-consuming, thought-consuming, most mystique-ridden training experience there is across academia and mental health systems.

I come back to my life several years later. There was mischief in the instructor's smile. He seemed to think his question humorous, like it contained a secret. It was an important question, posed ahead of a case conference course that was scheduled deep into the seminar year. These days I can be weary of these motivation-seeking overtures, suspicious of their purpose, being somewhere over halfway through my process, the learning process of "full" analytic training. I recall when training was first suggested to me, years ago now. It was suggested because I had not asked for it, nor even inquired after the training possibilities. I didn't know enough to ask, and that feels like a familiar disadvantage. See, there's deep background to this point: I'm an immigrant, arrived here as a 10-year-old from the United Kingdom back in the

20th century. My first day in an American school was tough. I felt like an outsider, but I wasn't a bereft foreigner for long. Speaking a common enough language and carrying a Disneyland-lover's prejudice, I soon accepted America on its own terms. I didn't know myself, but America didn't know itself either, so we got along fine. Anyway, the subject of analytic training first came up during a consultation hour with a colleague who had been a faculty member within a psychoanalytic psychotherapy group whose three-year training program I had completed a few years earlier. That previous training would qualify me for the next step, I was told.

"Have you considered full analytic training?" asked the woman whose time I leased twice a month for ongoing consultations. She'd asked her question with a slight conspiratorial whisper, which rendered her suggestions seductive. I was filled with buzzed curiosity. Do you know the good thing about whispering? No one can hear you. Do you know the bad thing about whispering? No one can hear you. I was thrown by the term she'd used. I often am when someone asks me something using a term or a phrase that I don't quite know the meaning of but only sort of know. It's not that I can't ask for clarification, but rather that I don't want to, thinking I should know what the term or phrase in question means, or that the person asking will be surprised or maybe disappointed that they must take a breath and explain their meaning. *Projections*, I will think, knowing that term's meaning, at least. *Danger*, perhaps. Regardless, I feel on these occasions a bit like Holden Caulfield from *Catcher in the Rye* when he makes bewildered observations about the inexplicable habits of people, or the strange detachment he feels from society as a whole. To tell you the truth, I don't want to go into it. I swear to God, I really don't. I feel like writing, and so I will, repeatedly.

"Full analytic training?" I asked gingerly. I braced myself for more terms or phrases I wouldn't know and might have to guess the meanings of. Acronyms. I dreaded the forthcoming onslaught of acronyms, the strange tongue of a new institutional milieu. However, my consultant was kind and patient, mostly because she was at that time only beginning full analytic training herself, which surprised me. I am inclined, the reader may soon guess, to place authority figures on pedestals, so it further throws me off when I learn that they are only halfway up a ladder to the pedestals I'd assumed they'd already reached. What was this particular pedestal? Again, I only sort of knew, and what I might have guessed was inflected with fantasies drawn from popular culture: full analytic training would be like some Jedi-Knight camp that one retreats to for some indefinite period, thus leading anxious friends and loved ones to whisper ominous questions and rumors to one another: *What's he been doing all this time? Is he coming back? We can't take on the Empire without him?* My consultant didn't promise me anything in particular with her proselytizing pitch. Nor did she flood me with acronyms pertaining to institutional bodies, use terms or phrases I didn't know, or perform an inventory of famous names, great minds that inhabited the family tree of psychoanalysis. Instead, she kept matters light and personal.

"I think you're looking for more," she said, placing emphasis on the word *more* and utilizing a technique that I'd associate with D. W. Winnicott though I couldn't quite summon to mind the term or phrase that denoted that technique. I knew that it has something to do with saying something that might provoke thought but not package it neatly, allowing the child/true self/patient to do the work that is theirs to do. I sort of know a lot of things like this. I'd sort of learned them first via that earlier three-year program. It was during that stretch that I read Freud for the first time, or at least read him for the first time properly, I should amend. In graduate school, nearly 30 years ago now, I'd been introduced to Freud, usually via secondary source material, coupled with lectures delivered by skeptical instructors who often curled their lips and stifled a sneer as they posted images of Sigmund on a PowerPoint display, or whatever existed prior to PowerPoint in the mid- to late 1990s (overhead projectors, I guess). The presentations that followed would be cursory, sketching out the range of Freudian theory, glancing at cultural context, culminating in thinly veiled derision. Freud was out of date. Freud emphasized drive theory too much, didn't understand women. I'd look at the image of Freud, one of those famous shots of him holding a cigar, dressed in tweed, and looking imperious. I'd learn to keep my own counsel on his lasting influence and remained reticent amid the female-centric atmosphere of graduate school. I didn't know much, didn't believe much, though I likely thought that Sigmund's cigar habit was a bad idea.

During that later three-year program, which taught a treatment method devised by Otto Kernberg and Heinz Kohut's contemporary James Masterson, I learned more about Freud and read a handful of his seminal texts. I was also introduced to the theories of Melanie Klein, plus her famous supervisees, the likes of Winnicott and attachment theory pioneer John Bowlby. There was also a touch of Wilfred Bion in the mix, as well as W. R. D. Fairbairn, largely because Masterson borrowed from the latter the idea of mapping an intrapsychic structure and linking it to personality disorder, or what he preferred to call disorders of self. I was becoming steeped in ego psychology, the observation of defensive structures, and further linking these theories to my burgeoning career, which had for some time congealed around the presenting problems of substance abuse and other addictions, including the controversially dubbed sex addiction, about which I'd eventually publish a book (amid analytic training no less!). By the time I was learning the Masterson model, I'd been working in hospital-based programs, residential group home settings, and concurrently in part-time private practice for about a decade. When I completed that course, I felt sated with training, for a while anyway. I was by then midcareer, spendthrift after a fair stretch of career investment. Meanwhile, I was shaping a protoanalytic identity as a versatile psychotherapist with a palette of theory and experience at my disposal, but with a bias toward confrontational stances, more often than not delivered to guilt-ridden or shamefaced patients who were as often as not mandated to hear what I had to say.

Was I dissatisfied? Did I want more, really? Likely, but I didn't know enough about what I didn't know. If you want to know the truth (yeah, a Holden turn of phrase), I sometimes think I've spent 30 years trying to consolidate ideas that I bring to mind, semi-articulate, usually not out loud, after which they drift away, draining away from memory and consciousness like dream content that leaves in the moments of waking. The goldfish state, I call this, as if forgetting were a natural phenomenon. At sporadic points in my career, I've had aha moments, checking boxes of previously thought notions as I'd hear them presented by someone else. I developed a package of knowns, aphoristic ideas that might grow in number or scope, though it might seem more like an organizational task than an open-minded exploration. Meanwhile, I was going about my working life, seeing clients, as I continued to call them, in various settings, though I clung to those of my apprenticeship: my intern and postintern years, my life as a near-grunt in the mental health hierarchy. Having understood some basics about a psychoanalytic framework, especially those "recommendations" about multiple sessions in a week in order to work on problems, I persistently asked why daily sessions, as in full 50-minute sessions, weren't a feature of the residential programs that employed me. I'd say things like, "Let me get this straight: We have a dozen or so patients in this program who are designated to stay for upward of a year. They live here. They live in the place we work. Tell me again why we can't have a training program for an in-depth therapy model that we could implement several days a week."

Such naivete. Medical or clinical directors with utilitarian minds would sigh and explain the obstacles to implementing such a plan, despite thinking it a good idea. I'd perceive an attitude, an elitist whiff they projected about psychoanalysis or anything that invoked its influence. They would allude to money matters, expanding caseloads of patients, the contracts that stipulated behavior modification strategies, triage-like assessment and interventions, and documentation requirements that would detail such methods. In treatment planning, they'd become obsessed with causality, ever asking why and how something had happened, but mostly so that it (whatever the *it* was) wouldn't happen again. These directors would use acronyms and dismiss the prospect I was raising. I would feel agreed with but patronized as they glanced at clocks, begging off further discussion but straining with their words to make me feel *heard*. Yeah, I wanted more. Ten years later, after I'd completed that Masterson model program, I wanted a similar, if still undefined, more. Loewald (1960) wrote of "something more" as a new identity with reality, as observed by a mediating analyst for a self-examining analysand. For me, this something more is to do with authority, peer systems: my perpetual sense of foreignness set against a hunger to belong. Yes, there's more to it than that. Prosaic matters emerged first. I still wasn't ready for the something more from a material standpoint—not enough savings. Of equal importance, I hadn't yet begun psychoanalysis, despite the earlier program, which hadn't required me to enter analysis per se, only therapy. I was and still am coy on this matter, thinking I've slipped by at times in life, across contexts. But with respect to psychoanalysis, no more. I've been in analysis for five years now, knowing less and less with each passing year, I think. I hope. The pop-Buddhist, inside mischief of that last thought will introduce a feature of this text, as will a degree of coyness about personal analysis, though I reserve the right to change my mind on this.

Of course, this book is not about my personal psychoanalysis, or that of my primary consultant for this book, a Portuguese psychologist named Pedro Job. That said, one's own psychoanalysis is inextricable from the training process, and it remains to be known (or not) how Pedro's and my endeavors in those immersions cross thresholds into our respective trainings in San Francisco, California, and Lisbon, Portugal. My life as an immigrant in-betweener has played out in some way that has repeated something not yet understood. Further, the social and professional intersections of our two countries are different, we've discovered. Pedro asserts that in Portugal psychoanalysis has a place in mainstream culture, that people across divides and walks of life seek analytic treatments. In America, I counter (I often say "America" to Europeans, less so to Americans), psychoanalysis is rarefied air and a rarely spotted animal in suburbia or rural towns. Or else it is deemed a relic, a onetime bridge between philosophy and medicine now obsolete to the concerns of a diverse, progressive society. My casual representation could be wrong. According to some, psychoanalysis is making a comeback and has been doing so for some time. But from my point of view, it still elicits ominous whispers or curt dismissals from many professionals and laypersons. It stirs fear, I think. It frightens the hell out of Pedro and me too, and we're into it—well into it, as in a no-turning-back-like feeling. No giving up.

On the matter of fear, it bears mentioning here that Pedro's and my training experience, and therefore the text of this book, has been broadly impacted by a public health crisis that barely has precedent in living memory: namely, the COVID-19 pandemic. It has also been moved and shaken by social undercurrents that have had accelerated impact in recent years—the #MeToo movement, the George Floyd incident of 2020, for example. In psychoanalytic training, I have been a member of an ironic minority: white, male, heterosexual. Amid a tense learning atmosphere, I am an imp, a watcher, a humble student, quietist and unaligned. At this prefacing stage, I will declare that I got started on this project before my consultant did, despite it being his idea originally. That was fair play, fair turnaround, as Pedro had gotten a head start otherwise, having started analysis and then analytic training before me. Later, I was the agitator, having talked so much with him about psychoanalysis in the years leading up to this project. We'd talked a lot, read a lot, taken tons of notes, agreed that he'd bring spiky activism to the book while I played the cool ironist. But we hadn't *written*. Enough, I complained. Time to write. To not write when having so much to say is not right. It is, at some point, well, literally unliterary. Pedro agreed, but he did so forlornly, declaring that he couldn't write with me because he hadn't the time and space for the project any longer due to personal circumstances. Plus, he didn't have the privilege of writing in his native tongue. This was late 2023, when Pedro became my erstwhile coauthor for this book. Oh well, I thought, feeling sympathetic but still chomping at the bit. So, in the spirit of analysis and literature, plus that of Pedro's good counsel in this task, I will quote Holden Caulfield more fully, drawing on a passage from *Catcher* where he is visiting an old school chum just prior to Christmas and drinking with him in a bar. Holden asks after the friend's father, knowing him to be a psychoanalyst. He says, "Suppose I went to your father and had him psychoanalyze me and all. What would he do to me? I mean, what would he do to me?"

Chapter 1
Transition to Analysis

From the outset, it has seemed that something shocking would emerge from psychoanalysis: some reminiscence cut from an old rock, born of sexual trauma (and possibly something else?), would rise to the surface and breathe. Only the breathing would be labored, and deeply flavored with a sour taste. Nausea. Revulsion. The *apres coup*, we learned to call this. Or afterwardness, or deferred action. Had we heard about that before, somehow known about it all along? Have we been shocked so far by our discoveries? By what we've learned about psychology, about ourselves, about what drives us, what stirs guilt, shame, or fear? And what about the communities we live and work in—about intersecting social conditions, temporal events, systems, intellectual and cultural traditions—the social unconscious that psychoanalysis also inhabits? Then there's Mother Earth, our shared original object. It's got its own problems. Lately, it's become addicted to hurricanes and big waves, is letting them loose more frequently. Maybe the Earth likes it, that swiftly moving, warm oceanic feeling. Maybe it's feeling down on itself, self-destructive, entropic. Actually, it's us. We did it. So, from the Earth's point of view, the problem's external. Lucky Earth. No guilt, unless it thinks it's done something wrong to deserve all of our abuse. What if we don't get the answers to our questions, about whether we've been right or wrong, or something in between. This is psychoanalysis, which doesn't feel down to Earth. What if we don't have a discovery? What if we seem more or less the same to others, to ourselves once the sinewy path of training is complete? Has psychoanalysis considered that: the value of not changing, or not changing much? From an average point of view, by which we mean a mooted canvasing of analytic opinion, we think that not changing significantly would mean that a patient/candidate-in-training wasn't done. If that's the case, we should keep going, whether accepted into the professional fold or not, until something really shocking occurs.

If and when it comes, this shocking experience, we might not want to see it, to deal with it, if it entails loss. Getting what you need has the fear of losing it built into it, writes Philips (1995)—the cost of wanting is the terror of losing, of not securing the future. We are reminded of earlier trainings, of where we came from, before we arrived at our institutes. Countertransference is important, we learned early. Perhaps it's the most important concept in analytic training, because it's about ourselves, and because it takes us back to early professional thoughts and before that to something deeply personal. It takes us back to school, then home. Then it bursts forward to those incipient professional moments. If you didn't think you could separate from your feelings well enough to sufficiently attend to the patient, then refer out. This is itself a derivative thought: strive for something, learn, but come to know your limits and ask for help, or else relinquish the task. That was a caveat we heard from our first mentors, supervisors, or senior peers, and before that from—I don't know—Dirty Harry, maybe: "Man's got to know his . . ." Limitations. Knowing them, adhering to them, would be the ethical thing to do, and psychotherapy, or psychoanalysis, would ever entail ethical choices. But what if we aren't aware of these "countertransference" phenomena. That countertransference is unconscious is the point, we might have been told. See, some of us had the impression that we *were* aware of such feelings such that we could make the decisions that supervisors warned about. Or, we weren't aware, having decided there was little we couldn't handle, or little that we shouldn't expect ourselves to handle. Suicidal patient? Bring it on, we thought audaciously. It's the kind of thing we're here for, isn't it? A sexual minority, or a patient from a foreign culture? Well, we'll adapt, ask questions, stay curious, and learn as we begin the work with such a person. A psychotic? We can get them to think properly, can't we?

In earlier trainings, as in nonanalytic trainings amid interdisciplinary staffing, supervisors were encouraging, at times risk-taking. They'd let us take difficult cases. Sometimes, regardless of our inclinations, they were more conservative, even squeamish if the context of a case was sensitive. A case of sexual abuse, with a patient of the opposite sex? Hmm . . . maybe not, we gleaned, especially if the therapist was male and the patient female. Heads would nod approvingly in management circles, tinged with dark murmurings. Too much history there to ignore, making prejudice in that singular context valid, as in acceptable. This recalls early psychoanalytic theory, seduction theory: the idea that mental illness results from sexual trauma, and the unconscious comes from reminiscences. In early training, we don't go there. Or we don't go there beyond early training, even in our thinking. We don't go to sex anymore, suggested Fonagy (2008), lamenting the trend. He'd researched the matter, using computer-assisted word frequency analysis to study the number of terms pertaining to sex in psychoanalytic literature over a number of recent years. They were lacking, basically. Perhaps this is a matter of expertise, of really knowing what we're doing. Or it's little to do with knowledge in a conventional, positivistic sense. It's a matter of taking care, of greater levels of sensitivity infiltrating our profession—a paradigm shift, as some like to put it.

At an agency with a hierarchical system, the assignment of cases might be subject to fate, depending on the demographics. Gender, age, race, patient acuity are all factors in the matching of patients and therapists, problems matched with expertise or levels of experience. Meanwhile, a question rings out to the budding professional: What is your countertransference—what feelings, stirred by the presenting problem, by the person you've been asked to treat, spring from your past? The question about countertransference elicits an impulse to shrug, a desire to brush off a troublesome idea: that we might not be able to handle it, whatever *it* is. Perhaps we are not so much incapable or lacking requisite experience but rather inhibited. We are scared. And we know, or we'll have learned at some point, that this wisdom emerged from Freud's evolving idea of transference in the early 1900s; he wrapped notions of repression around a pivotal idea: we turn away from reality, seeking pleasure (Freud, 1911). We want pleasure, or at least relief from pain, when we seek treatment for ourselves. We want to feel better and to feel safe with a therapist, hence psychotherapy for the consumer's desire and, problematically, for that of the therapist. Analysis is different, we understand. It won't feel better, ultimately. It'll be an *apres coup*: something once experienced if not understood is followed by a moment of understanding that disturbs and reverses time. It will revive some original agony, as Winnicott (1974) put it. But it's okay, says a metatraining instruction. As a would-be analyst, you don't have to be an expert, an all-knowing, omnipotent object, in order to help. That thing about expertise: it's a croc of . . . you know. That's some relief, actually. It's just ironic that it emerges from the most rigorous training model across mental health systems.

Back to School

You want to know how rigorous? Well, differences across institutions notwithstanding, full analytic training programs entail a four-year seminar, typically, or didactic teaching component—linearly or nonlinearly proceeding, depending on the program, whether it's in the United States or elsewhere. Historically, seminar was a multiple-day-per-week commitment comprised of classes, reading assignments, and participation in case conferences wherein candidates would present verbatim notes from sessions to peers and a facilitating faculty member. At the San Francisco Center for Psychoanalysis (SFCP), seminar is currently a one-day-per-week commitment consisting of three back-to-back

90-minute classes stretched over a 9-month academic year, times four. This is one component of a tripartite training system known as the Eitingon model. The other two components are a candidate's personal (or training) analysis and the supervised treatment of cases. The reading in seminar is prodigious, but a saving grace is that no examinations are given; no "pop quizzes," to borrow American parlance. Once a year, candidates are subject to a progression evaluation, presided over by a committee, which discusses a candidate's performance in terms of participation, whether that is deemed active or passive, cooperative, insightful—in rarer cases, perhaps, whether it is considered disruptive in some way. Institutional cultures vary in these respects, with some allowing or compelling in-person interviews for progression evaluations, which include presentations and such. Some institutions don't have a formal seminar program; rather, classes are taken at a candidate's discretion, with personal analysis and supervision of cases being privileged in a training experience. This kind of system exists in France, for example. Regardless, whether in the United States or elsewhere, seminar is not the priority training ground. Seminar performance is not the priority criteria. Performance with one's patients takes that mantle.

Would-be candidates apply to psychoanalytic institutions months, sometimes a year or so, ahead of training onset. In that phase, they traverse a series of interviews with established faculty, presenting verbatim notes from patient sessions as an incipient performance of that norm and in addition providing a more personal interview. Upon acceptance, the applicant becomes a training candidate, embarks on the seminar course, and upon institutional approval (during the first year of training usually) finds a clinical supervisor from the well-networked analytic community and chooses a case for psychoanalytic treatment. A case in which a clinician meets with a patient three or more (usually four or sometimes five) times per week over two years is designated as psychoanalytic and requires approval by a supervisor; this is dubbed a control case, of which three are needed in order to graduate from a program. Also, the candidate will need separate supervisors to meet with weekly for each control case, to whom the candidate will submit annual reports about their own analytic development plus rigorously conceptual and vignette-laden reports about the development of control case patients. At a later point in a candidate's process, at least two of those cases will need to overlap chronologically—a stage of training called "immersion." As suggested earlier, training norms can vary across institutions, and candidates needn't be rigidly linear. People take time off or slow their pace for various reasons. This is reputedly more common in Europe. Pedro, for example, chose a supervisor for a control case who wasn't yet qualified at the onset of their work together, so he had to wait a year for his case to start counting, so to speak, toward its two-year completion. That isn't necessarily a commonplace occurrence. Personally, I think Pedro is nuts.

You can lose touch with day-to-day society in this immersion. You're not just in seminar; you are seminarian, semi-cloistered. You have thinning awareness of current events, external happenings, even as you are chastised about your ignorance, admonished, as the psychoanalytic establishment has been admonished, to pay more attention to what's happening in the streets. Okay, so you once thought for a minute that Nikki Haley was the opening act on the last Taylor Swift tour—anyone can make that kind of mistake. But not knowing about . . . everything? That's a problem, and you shouldn't have to wait for graduation to reenter the "real" world: I mean, the real world of Listserve threads, the travails of a favorite sports team, the dinner theater of contemporary politics, the breaking news alerts on our internet home pages; what's John Oliver or John Stewart talking about in any given week? On the matter of graduation, a candidate graduates from SFCP if he, she, or they complete the seminar component, meet requirements for approval of each control case, and—upon finishing seminar—also produce a theoretically driven clinical paper that would be deemed publishable in a peer-reviewed academic journal, whether a candidate chooses to pursue that route or not. Whether these evaluative norms are fair, equitable, or accurate in what they seek to achieve is open to debate, which is understandably fraught with tension within and across institutes. In the United States, the governing body that oversees all of this from a distance, granting psychoanalytic accreditation to programs and providing recommendations for candidate standards, is the American Psychoanalytic Association (APsaA). The international body disseminating standards and recommendations for training is the International Psychoanalytic Association (IPA).

It's interesting how analytic training programs stick candidates in groups first, blending relationship with authority to that which lurks within a peer system. The bosom of peer support is a presumed balm alongside an evaluative setup that is steadily delivered over the course of years. A candidate meets fellow candidates, most of whom are friendly while some seem wary or truculent, sharing where they are from, where they practice and with what kinds of patients, whether they are a they and not a he or a she. As new candidates meet one another within an institution for the first time, we might wonder about shadow groups: those who wanted in but were rejected; those who know about analytic training but want no part of it and never will; curious in-betweeners, the would-be converted. Going forward, candidates repeat introductory exercises at the beginning of each seminar class given the modest numbers (a group of a half dozen is deemed optimal), though the process of "getting to know one another" may subside in subsequent seminar years. The ritual yields to a weary observation that says something like, *Shouldn't we be sharing something else, like one's developing voice, the emerging "analytic" identity?* The introductions stir the pots of envy, of competition, and also the desire to fit in—our fears of group menace. Some of us had negative experiences with groups when younger, with play friends or at various stages of school. Some continued that trend into college and then in graduate school, then in the "psychoanalytic psychotherapy" programs that are the kiddy pools leading to full analytic training, and lastly in the marathon of training itself.

For seminar, which is the paradigm of learning that is most recognizable to the average student of anything, candidates are placed in cohorts, so called to indicate our roughly shared goals and characteristics. We are psychoanalytic training candidates, accepted as capable professionals, worthy of further training, and deemed able to navigate the lengthy, rigorous path that psychoanalytic training demands. In truth, we are a motley group drawn from diverse backgrounds. We have different needs, varied levels of psychoanalytic knowledge or clinical experience, and differing expectations for learning. And different personalities. In an average group, one or two are cliquey, supercilious, and guarded, having struggled already with the institution, which demands a realpolitik that shirks argument, expects collegial decorum. These candidates are discerning intellects, wicked smart, a bit too cool for school. Hotshots, Holden would have called them. Deemed prickly, as in sensitive, they are sensitive to being called sensitive, thinking this a microaggression: an assignment of thin skin that dismisses fair complaint. Other candidates seem nervous but affectively contained, keeping a lid on angst, not sure they will fit into the group or keep up with program demands. This candidate type is not in training to stir the pot of change. They just want to be psychoanalysts. In any group, there needs to be one who will speak up and stir discussion, whether they represent the whole or not. This figure is cheerfully candid and openhearted; volunteering of biases, having already selected their theoretical darlings; uncensored in opinion, half assuming like-mindedness when punctuating an idea that is politically inflected. As a whole, we'd rather talk about authority, the "other" that is the institute to which we don't yet fully belong. We might not feel belonging in our cohorts, so we'll either bail out and join another group or else soldier on, still eager if reticent. We're not going to go into it, if you want to know the truth, because groups are dangerous, Freud (1921) wrote. Group derivatives—tribes, nations, families, institutes, cohorts—may ostracize us, or take us in but cut us down to size.

Well, what isn't dangerous? Families are dangerous. That's a group. Society is dangerous. Institutions, movements are dangerous. The Earth is dangerous. We are dangerous. As candidates, we have ideas born of life experience, education, and professional careers so far. We'll be hard to teach given that we've been here before, having at least thought about almost every concept that will be laid before us. We've idealized this thing called psychoanalysis to the degree that we will properly engage, but we won't be talked down to—we're not novices or kids. Well, we are kids, the new kids on the block of psychoanalysis. Indeed, some of us will feel like infants longing to be cared for, held in an environment of Winnicottian love. But we won't be bossed around, rebuked if we're not speaking up enough, or chastised if we're running late to class. In our bristling resistance, we'll place the curriculum in our crosshairs first. Review courses? We'll sniff disdainfully at those. A reading of Freud, of "Mourning and Melancholia" (1917), or *Three Essays* (1905), or *The Ego and the Id* (1923). Fine. They're all classics. We've read them before and they bear reading again and discussing. But what about *Interpretation of Dreams* (1900), or at least its famous chapter 7. See, we knew already that it was important, that chapter. But did the institute's curriculum committee know that we knew? Why not a full course on dreams? Can you call it "full" analytic training if it doesn't contain a course entirely devoted to dreams?

The more modernist among us may bemoan inattention to mirror neurons as much as the lack of dream interpretation. Some might think that Rizzolatti and Gallese ought to be studied as much as Freud, or that papers by Beebe, Solms, Schore, Damasio, LeDoux, to name-drop a few from the realm of neuroscience, should be as famous as anything by the old patriarch. Others want theoretical resurrections, once-eclipsed figures like Sandor Ferenczi or Hans Loewald brought in from the cold and studied anew. Springboarding from reading the once marginal, this student faction wants relevance assigned to social forces that surround psychoanalysis. Society stimulates drives. Social structures drive angst, so they'll want Erich Fromm on the reading lists for classes, plus the odd work by Harry Stack Sullivan. And this should set the stage for feminist theory, queer theory, reading the likes of Jessica Benjamin, Carol Gilligan, Judith Butler, or for delving into the variably termed intersubjective or relational schools of psychoanalysis, wherein egalitarianism, co-constructed ideas between clinician and patient in the analytic space, is a mooted virtue. Therefore, Nancy Chodorow, Robert Stolorow, or Stephen Mitchell should make the curriculum cut. Psychoanalysis intersects with economics, with politics, and so we have a social unconscious in which class, gender, and racial bias live, and we must think and talk about these biases. We must read Beverly Stoute and think about Black rage. We must platform a protest against a sclerotic orthodoxy. Meanwhile, amid this charter, we shall read the personal journals of Marion Milner and interpret the squiggling figures of Winnicott's children.

In conscious time, as in the course of four years, the organization of courses reflects a sampling of biases drawn from the interests and knowledge of a go-to or long-gone-to pool of instructors. A centralized ego, mired in some manner of conflict, is apparent if one is brave enough to attend curriculum meetings that are weirdly open to candidate input. The topics of instruction range and intertwine, reflecting old guards but also new forces moving in: the body and the ego; drive, motivation, and affect; memory and trauma; transference and the compulsion to repeat; internalization; the abiding existence of a social unconscious; infant observation. We listen cautiously, perhaps distrustfully, to instructors who speak of a biologically delineated unconscious, locatable in the brain if not the mind. We're more familiar with a theory of dynamic unconscious, of things unknown because of internal conflict that cannot be located via mental geography. We're not sure how relevant neuroscience is to psychoanalysis. We are reminded that mental representation, whereby one thing can *stand* for another, transforms drive, perception, and memory and determines our experience. We consolidate knowledge that repression was once the cornerstone of psychoanalytic theory, though we speak at length about patients suffering from trauma, accompanied by more rigid defenses: states of dissociation, psychic numbing, and hyperarousal. We knew already, or we had felt from our patients already, that some trauma had been prolonged, even chronic, and multiply determined. We came to understand that, for some, traumatic memory is not absent due to repression but had never been established properly in the first place.

A place of learning, a building, holds levels of group character and history. The ego is a body ego, and brick and mortar exude an organized mind. There is little evidence of traumatic or psychotic collapse, at least not in the place where we first gathered to learn. Approaching a psychoanalytic institute that has a face and a physical presence stirs a queasy if intrigued shudder. At first glance, an edifice of certain age juxtaposes its features: there is a corrugated screen that closes over a front entrance, resembling that of a mechanic's workshop or a storage unit. Softly colored red bricks are sandwiched by aging cement, part of an architect's vision that might have dreamed ivy branches twining. Instead, the trim on the doorway, around the windows, and upon the bars that protect from a ghetto encroachment are all inky black, classic psychoanalytic black. There is an anonymity about this place. Nowhere is there a conspicuous banner emblazoned with the institute's logo. It has an austere warehouse quality, like the empty loft space of a profiteering developer, the domicile of a secret society or a criminal guild. Its dignity suggests history, an enduring presence. The doorway is a quaint inlet, sheepishly pulled back from the side street and barely separated from stains of human waste that signal a transient culture nearby. Yes, psychoanalysis is part of the community, just about. It is ensconced within fentanyl city, blocks away from opioid ground zero, yet divorced from that topical scourge. It is community based, as in there for anyone to walk up to, to see and to smell, but then turn away from, barely curious.

Inside, there is a doorman/person, an unnecessary figure perhaps, stolidly monitoring the impressive yet riches-lacking premises from a shadowy nook. He opens the door to anyone who looks respectable but can't negotiate the entry code below the speaker or who shows evidence of the institutional prestige that pulled them to this address. That's a few steps away, amid the crimson-tinged light of a foyer that is flanked by a wall of names on shiny marble. These are the donors, the people who are making much of this possible. It's almost enchanting. It looks like a war memorial, like we're meant to bow or at least pause before it and genuflect. Pushing forward, a visitor might cast an anthropological eye on a space that funnels into a mouthy auditorium, though it all seems economically designed, cut from the mind of a square personality. The compact rooms on the first floor are there for supervision, for seminar, and are situated in a neat rectangle, separated from an administrative heart. That's upstairs, beating away quietly among a few digital riches: computers, some office ware, plus stray domestic elements like a microwave, a discarded coffee cup or two, some crumbs left over from the lunchtime meeting of the psychoanalytic education division or progressions committee. Even in here there is some analytic ephemera: a bust of Freud is tucked in a corner on a counter, looking like it's on hold between a museum and an antique shop. On the walls of the stairs and in a break room there is a big-screen TV available for videoconferencing, plus reverent portraits of esteemed alumni or once-visiting professors. The one with the woman sitting with a cigarette, gazing outward, is Betty Joseph, some newcomer guesses.

Disruption

Before COVID gave us a scapegoat for the flaws of analytic training, or a nickname for all that was altering society, having a live interactive experience within our offices, with colleagues with whom we share an aggregate of a hundred words over the course of a year, was something most of us took for granted. Congregating at this cozy downtown institution, gathered together in a room in the afterglow of program acceptance, was something we hadn't taken for granted but certainly looked forward to. Is there such a thing as measured awe, of suspended gratitude? If there is, then psychoanalytic training institutions are among those entities that elicit such feelings. Back-to-school night. If a body catch a body, then this body ego will hold us together, catch us if we edge toward a cliff and start to fall off. Or did the Robert Burns poem read, "If a body meet a body," referring to something less wholesome or heroic happening between people? Some of us had dreamed of this thing, saved money for it, argued with friends and family over it. You're going to do what? More school? Psychoanalytic training? Is that like a doctorate? Will there be more letters after your name, more numbers on the checks, preferably some extra zeros? The short answers would be unsatisfactory, the long ones inexplicable. They won't have asked deeper questions, like whether it would be a profound career- and life-changing endeavor, much less a slide down infantile fantasy: a nuzzle up to a bosomy, oceanic feeling. Back on solid if inflamed or soggy earth, and regarding the thing about money and numbers, the trajectory might travel sideways for a while, possibly backward, we'll have said. In fact, over the long term, volunteerism beckons; that is, if teaching is an option, that might also apply to supervisory duties the way some things are going.

Not promising, at least not of material joy. Debt and poverty loom if we really screw this thing up. Oh well, there will be other kinds of riches on offer, of a kind we'd be encouraged to put words to eventually. There are words or phrases that place thought on the idea that we ought not find singular terms or succinct phrases to define phenomena. Words like *reductionism* and *reification* come to mind, and get said a lot. Upon acceptance, we heartily agreed with the ethic of discovery without conclusion, of thought without foreclosure. The funny thing is that our psychoanalytic institutes live in a material world and are therefore not immune to the contagion of shorthand, though most acronyms are administrative in meaning. They are invoked by organizational staff who may be impervious to psychoanalytic reach, the calories of its work quite foreign to them. Also, there are those who straddle the clinical and administrative silos. They have risen within the ranks, assimilated institutional culture and tongues, but kept muscular feet in the doors of business. They are financially literate people shepherding the institute's material existence. From the pews, a candidate might observe analytic culture, notice norms pertaining to business structure, notions of pedagogy, of group organization. Soon the illusion of uniqueness, of immunity from external phenomena, dissolves. Ominously, the contagion of COVID-19 crept into view in the dawn of 2020 with a growing ubiquity of mask wearing on commuter buses and trains, backgrounded by memories of former biological acronyms and nicknames: swine and SARS, for example. The local Asian population seemed scarred by this history, appearing especially attentive to cautionary measures in public settings.

We were not immune. Soon thereafter, something astonishing—something truly shocking, though not emerging from psychoanalysis—occurred. We lost something. We were told to stay away. We were told this about our institute, whose impressive ephemera would now gather dust for an indeterminate spell. So much for that measured awe. Gratitude, too, would be placed on hold. Far beyond the reach of institutes, we were barred from buses and trains, and to some extent from supermarkets, which were running out of supplies anyway. The museums closed; so too the libraries, the music venues, the event centers that hosted conferences that some of us were due to attend. We were told to stay away from schools, from all public gatherings, and from hospitals unless we had COVID itself, but not even then if we had symptoms and there weren't enough beds. We left our offices behind, stayed home and signed up for something called Zoom, and told our patients that telehealth was the frame of treatment for the time being. We mothballed our recently purchased couches, were barred

from theaters and restaurants, barred from bars, even, for a cosmic minute. If you were a contented loner amid this turmoil, you shrugged, sympathized, but adapted quickly. Only the lonely, plus those whose working lives compelled the "live," suffered. Having just started our training months earlier, my cohort and I awaited instructions on what to expect. We stayed in our pajamas and signed on for the next week's classes, and when our programs changed, we clicked on our links, half grateful for all the techies whose skills would keep the flame of civilization alive. The moment felt Promethean, Pandoran, a preview of the AI revolution that is now upon us. Gathered in virtual rooms, plunged into a once only imagined future, we gazed at a "gallery" of faces, all of whom loomed back with twitchy anxiety, wondering how to continue now that the body had gone. It felt like Rome was burning, that dystopia had arrived overnight. The people in the streets, those incurious passersby near the vacated center: some would bark out their suddenly not-so-crazy ideas, still claiming the apocalypse was nigh, only now to more credulous listeners.

What has psychoanalysis had to say about earthy disasters that portend greater doom but are currently at bay for most of us? About a pandemic that is at hand for everyone, or about other social crises that encircle us? As an institution, or a living force, what has it thought, done, or given, besides its stalwart endurance, its survival? As candidates, we glean its social ethos from its modest economic presence, from its air of perpetual abstaining. This extends to the prevailing work ethic, a spirit of volunteerism. Volunteers are the strange cogs of institutional tradition, for volunteerism would seem antithetical given Freud's (1913) teachings about the importance of a professional, fee-paying service that would protect patient and analyst from delusions about motive. The analyst should not impose his views or his charity. The patient, or analysand, should not be in doubt as to why the clinician is performing the work. This is not charity. This is not even a cause in any conventional sense—a social movement, as some might think. It is a service, one that should be taken seriously and therefore should be a paid endeavor. So why not apply a similar ethic to pedagogical services? Why do we ask seminar instructors to spend months (in all likelihood) gathering data, poring over old papers, devising a curriculum, copying pages and turning some into pdfs, and then, finally, creating a lesson plan plus a strategy of how to engage a fledgling group of analytic training candidates for six-to-nine-week courses without paying them a good old-fashioned dime for their efforts? Meanwhile, we recruit training and supervising analysts, likely the cream of the institutional crop, asking them to charge downwardly flexible fees for training candidates for an indeterminate yet protracted stretch of years. Are we like average American communities in the contemporary age: Do we not like teachers?

If levels of volunteerism decline, or the availability of supervisors starts to wane, perhaps due to derisorily low fees they are pressured to accept, then psychoanalytic institutes might come to resemble another systemic force that Freud rejected: religion. Because, in the absence of material rewards, only the devout will remain. Perhaps institute principals might want it this way, being prudes about money. Maybe this is what the collective voice in psychoanalytic communities is saying, to its patients and colleagues: only stick around, give your time, energy, and diving in deep capacity if you really want to, not because it pays the bills, or might later pay the bills if teaching generates supervisees that would pay or patient referrals. That teaching helps to expand a practice is an old supposition, and not one that is exclusive to psychoanalysis. Indeed, it may seem at a casual glance that psychoanalysis is behind on the curve of professionals who springboard from teaching to private practice success. Psychoeducational gurus, exponents of short-term treatment models, seem to have a marketing edge, are miles ahead of analytic thinkers in the gaping internet classroom. Webinars are the thing, making conference rooms and live classes seem obsolete. Shared screens are in, whiteboards are long gone, and the dry erase pens are all dry. The one thing that the live versus the virtual will have in common is a desire to be loved, and here volunteerism should be an equalizer, because everyone should love a volunteer, shouldn't they? Kiss me, says the badge, or is that for voting? Anyway, that's also voluntary, also endangered.

When an institute of higher learning tries to balance a need to attract volunteers with a desire to elicit honest feedback between students and teachers with an eye toward optimal program experience, increased understanding of student needs, plus protections that allow for anonymous expression of opinion, then . . . well, we're not sure that psychoanalytic education divisions really thought about what they were getting us into. Had they not noticed the influence of social media on how we all relate to one another? In designing online portals that send out surveys, with seven-deep question palettes that inquire after-class curriculum, teacher performance, fellow student (or group interaction performance), plus suggestions as to how each class might improve, while trying to keep secure each respondent's identity, programs are asking for something that may have been less pronounced in the era of pen and paper. Clicking fingers might generate more caustic comments than a tired hand straining with ancient cursive. Hitting "submit" may ignite a buzz of aggression much more than the polite laying down of a sheet by the side of a teacher's table. Some may think that the candidate pool has changed, that expectations of instructors are higher, and that skin is thinner. The age of the genteel is gone. If the lesson plan feels phoned in, the testy, demanding student of today will say so, even if the teacher is a volunteer, because seminar is expensive and still happens in business hours, and whether the time of the instructor is paid for or not, the hours spent learning come at an opportunity cost.

That's a rationale, a tacit excuse for writing your worst when the calls for review are made. And one other thing: sending out the grading commentary for the teacher and, to a much lesser extent, for one's peers is easier from the quiet of a remote space, far from the shifty looks of an assembled group. Or put it another way: in one sense, nothing has changed. Anonymous feedback from students about the efficacy of a course and its teacher is nothing new, but as many psychoanalytic thinkers are cautioning to those seeking reifications, the matter is not so simple. So what's the issue here? What's the implied indictment of a system that accommodates the digital age, has been disrupted by public events, and with them a social, state, and cultural sanctioning of social distancing? We're suggesting that distance has made all the players in our educational field less patient, or less confident, and thus more tentative in approach, in our forbearance. We're adding that isolation, and to some extent social deprivation, has agitated our unconscious aggression, made us cagey and restless or passively resistant. Regarding the wider internet community, Kravis (2017) writes:

> If you picture the hundreds of millions of people around the world who at this very moment are staring at the screens of their devices, then you realize that in a way all the choices are the same, because the people looking at the screen are becoming the same (Russo, 2005, p. 18). Sameness not only averts envy; it also facilitates the discharge of aggression, for, as Bion (1961) realized, some forms of hostility are best expressed anonymously, preferably cloaked by the homogeneity of large-group membership.

We can do what we like in front of a laptop in our own homes, in our internet classrooms. In transient moments, we can click on a button and blacken our screens or mute ourselves. We are children in our playpens, with a TV-like window to the outside world. There are no instances of squeezing past others' chairs, edging quietly outside a door when we need a trip to the bathroom. At breaktime, there is no garrulous chatter or awkward conversing by the coffee machine, depending on how that norm transpired for each person BC (before COVID).

Reading Gabbard (2020) at the height of the COVID crisis, one might have thought that the pandemic intrusion would bring us closer together, that it would inspire levels of esprit de corps at our institutions, or within our cohorts at least. With patients, there was tentative but then committed accommodation. Though opinions varied as to the necessity of restrictions, polite cooperation plus a sense of mutual caretaking prevailed whenever someone reported feeling exposed to the virus, whether testing positive or not. A session might be postponed pending a result. Masks would be worn if meeting live, or else a phone or Zoom session would substitute for the hour. Whatever ill feelings or judgments that existed were sidelined. A crisis was upon us. It was no time to be imputing defensiveness because of fears. Gabbard writes that the virus altered the analytic frame: he found himself having discussions with patients about the latest stories on viral research. Patients worried about catching the virus from their analysts, and vice versa. A session would begin with, "How are you?" with expanded meaning. Everyone was in the same boat with respect to this unprecedented problem. No one's life was untouched by it, so no endeavor, psychoanalysis included, would be unaffected. Striking a spiritual tone, Gabbard adds, "The pandemic is a random occurrence taking place in an inexplicable setting over which we have no control" (2020, p. 1094). Invoking Camus's *The Plague*, he asks, "Do we live in a godless universe where no one can come to our rescue?" The phrase "inexplicable setting" draws special curiosity as an inexplicable thought in itself. It conjures something beyond a physical space and time—more like a baffling, overdetermined phenomena that has overwhelmed our collective thinking.

In keeping with that thought, it seems wrong to blame institutional malaise on pandemics or internet trends. For a wider range of overdetermined phenomena—meaning those that have so many possible causes—analytic candidates like us are feeling less a part of, having less of a fellow feeling, and we may be more pissed about our situation than we realize, because we remember that "wanting more" hunger we had before training began. But we were stuck, and now we are frozen, having gotten comfortable in our unsatisfactory states, satisfied to complain and scapegoat, take out our smoothed-out misery on some visible figure who magnetizes us but appears to block access to the quorum of planning and decision. Or these visible figures (supervisors, teachers) might point vaguely toward the engine room but have little to offer if we reply that we've been to that office already and found it impermeable. The teachers, they smile, say good morning, give of their time and work, but we resist giving back, not forgiving the imperfections that permeate this exercise. We didn't come here to give but to receive, we now protest, sometimes silently. We want our money's worth, if not for the particular hour or so before us then for all time and effort that culminated in our arrival at this now disrupted moment of our careers. So we may seem to be looking back at teachers, not even hoping anymore that they will contain our flattened airs, our dying rage, but rather expecting them to resuscitate us and blow wind into our flailing sails. We want them to be interesting, confident, and relaxed, to say something Freudian, Lacanian, Kleinian, Bionian, Winnicottian, Aristotelian—maybe Franciscan—or something even more cryptic that will tease our thinking and pull it forward, and then we might do the rest, in studied disagreement at times but generally singing the same tune, having read the same stuff beforehand and kept up with a broadly prescribed pace. That's the party we came for and want to keep going until dawn.

> **"What keeps you from saying something?" This was my analyst, getting ahead of me with her presumptions, referring to the deadness of my voice. "I volunteer a lot," I retort, sounding defensive, which she also duly points out. She's doing her job, the kind of job I want to do, apparently. I continue, pointing to my participation record in case conference: "I give," I say, half quoting a grateful instructor's line to his presenters. "I ask questions, make comments, express myself." I sound like a teenager protesting a bad grade. A pause follows. It's time to admit something in that knowingly left-open gap: "Okay, I haven't said anything about the disparity in participation. There's obviously a split between those who have much to say and a faction that sits quietly, saying as little as possible. One or two make excuses, or they say something verbose, just to get by. There's a candidate who just sits there saying nothing like he's stuck in Saturday traffic school, forced to be there. Sometimes I respect his attitude, his gnomic silence. It feels like a protest. The rest of us look similarly jaded in our semiprofessional wear, stuck in our makeshift home office spaces. We're like Kafkaesque beetles lying off to the side, starting to smell. Thank God for Zoom and social distancing." This last bit was a joke, obviously. My analyst didn't laugh. She never laughs. She has no sense of humor as far as I can tell. We disagree about humor, only she doesn't believe in disagreements either. In psychoanalysis, disagreements are called enactments. "Nobody says anything about the class dynamic. So it's like nothing is happening," she eventually comments. "You go along with the charade, acting like nothing is happening." "We're all a bunch of phonies," I say in a mock Holden voice, or what I imagine was his voice. Again, no laugh, though my analyst may have wondered whether I was being earnest or merely sardonic.**

So the problem of teaching, whether a matter of pedagogical styles or of curriculum choices that don't reflect enough theoretical depth or sociocultural focus or cultural sensitivity, didn't only manifest online. Some voted with their feet, not showing up, in layers: choosing to stay on Zoom even after the COVID crisis subsided and restrictions had been lifted, participating minimally in classes, sometimes absenting themselves entirely. At times seminar felt like an unannounced strike—a passive withdrawal from institutional authority, and even more passively, perhaps, from a conformist peer group. As candidates within thrust-together cohorts, we had our opportunities to talk it through, decide on a cohesive response, or else comment in disparate pieces from within cliques or only to those we found trustworthy or like-minded. We agreed on some things, the easiest, like whether early seminar classes were too remedial to meet our ambiguously shared needs. We had no problem stroking the group ego. If discouraged, we'd indulge in a little gallows humor, usually at authority's expense. We'd agree that a certain teacher said that one thing, plus one or two other things, was a problem and needed dealing with. The written word here is reticent. The expanded topic would cover racism, cultural and generational divides. The incidents that cleaved opinion, rendering some mutinous, were partly about individual actions, but whether they constitute institutional rot is the stiffly debated debatable. The issue is a Gordian knot, tied with illusion and disillusionment. It brings to mind a famous quote often attributed to Winston Churchill, to which we might add a twist: "Psychoanalytic training is the worst model of teaching for the treatment of the human mind . . . except for all the others."

Today, we wander about the bodies of our respective institutes in San Francisco, Lisbon, and elsewhere. Until recently, they seemed like carcasses, metonymic of fixtures left standing amid disorder. In Lisbon, the institute is situated at the base of a highrise. From the outside it looks glassy and dark inside, abandoned, unremarkably furnished but sturdily designed, maybe at risk of being squashed, but more likely holding the weight of what's above. We don't know. There's no basement, anyway. There's an executive suite, maybe, on a top floor where the president of the institute's office lies, not in the building's ass where the candidates go, naturally. The San Franciscan edifice has had an upgrade or two—off to the side. There's a newly manicured park adjacent to the building, spotted with benches, a modern art indulgence in the shape of a druidic sickle. At the outset of our training, just prior to COVID, this area was in shambles due to urban development of a business-as-usual variety. Now it's transformed, looks reborn. Graffiti mars or beautifies the back wall of the center, depending on one's taste and sensibility. To the north and south are towering new highrises, one an apartment complex, the other a techie ghetto. The dive bar that is kitty-corner to the institute is still there, having survived the pandemic's economic hits. Alcohol usually does. There are still only a few people around, in or out of the building. Inside, the live attendance is sparse, the give and take of volunteerism, employment, and training seems tentatively present, its wheels still grinding. New technology has been brought in to aid the hybrid experience, or coax some people back. The "owl," as it is called, is a motion camera situated in the center of a conference room, there to keep an eye on everything.

Like nothing is happening? A lot is happening, actually. New normal will return to old normal perhaps, with live instruction and conferences back on the schedule next year (as in required) if not this one. Lots of voices are being heard. A lot is being talked about, but also enacted, no doubt, for the talking is in isolated pockets, with messages, sometimes of disgusted resignation, later dispatched on a Listserve in edited form with the revulsion culled from the manifest content. The reader of emails must read like they might listen to a resistant patient or to a dream. We must glean from what is expressed—that someone or something is not feeling included—but also think about what is not being shared. But we are all conscientious people, we all defensively agree. Good hearts, good minds. Not that long ago, we were just getting started with our psychoanalytic learning experience. Now we feel like jaded elders already. We need a break, a tune-up, a kick in the ass . . . something. We care about the future of psychoanalysis, what it might stir in the unconscious of individuals, facilitating greater understanding, some manner of improvement in their lives; we care about the future of our communities, and even consider how psychoanalysis might coax more people into its ever-evolving mission. It will have to sort some things out first: that means dispelling some prejudices about its utility; it means acknowledging shortcomings, noticing that things aren't like how they used to be, or even how we thought they were. If we walk to the end of the street of our center, we'd enter a milieu that doesn't know we exist, though we are a part of it. We might observe attractive, lively—if smelly—urban life, thriving, suffering, surviving. Or not. We might see asses being actually kicked or knees upon necks and feel moved to say something or to call someone. Nothing like that happens near our center, as far as we know. We don't see it. We didn't see it. We left our offices, our work communities, and went home. We saw the video online.

Chapter 2
Inclusion and Numbers

"Nothing happened," I said in supervision. After saying that nothing is happening, and then declaring that thought itself an illusion because it seemed that much was being talked about, albeit in separate isolated pockets, "silos" as people keep calling them, I had to say that, as far I was concerned, *nothing*—as in nothing of substance—had been talked about. "Hmm," my supervisor uttered, thinly curious, keeping any skepticism close to his chest. "Why do you think it was like that?" It was refreshing to have someone appear to believe me, to not challenge my premise with, *Hmm . . . what makes you say nothing happened?* I wouldn't have welcomed that kind of challenge, but I wouldn't have bristled at it either. I was in training, which means I would have been used to having my assumptions examined. And I would have rolled with the tension, the gnarly feeling in my stomach as I conjure words of explanation, which means self-defense—the need to back up my assertion versus pausing to realize that a red light has appeared—coupled with a suggestion: it's time to look at yourself.

Nothing like that happened in this moment. My supervisor seemed to be with me, on my side, leaving space for discussion of anything related to training, whether that was coursework, the progress of control cases, or in this case the mini-culture of training itself; he seemed to readily accept what many had reported before, that the best laid plans of discussion and exploration in groups go more than awry. Supervision: it's not like analysis, only it is about analysis. Being a candidate: it's not like being an analysand, though transferences emerge that are similar—the tendency to idealize, to project authority and an envious withholding instead of kindly mentorship. In the moment—that "this" moment, so described—I was speaking of program matters that were peripheral to my training, which itself seems theoretically suspect. Peripheral

> **matters? That's like a dream that one asserts is irrelevant before it's been thought about. What's more accurate is that my material was peripheral to what I think a candidate should think about and present to a supervisor. As a result, my descriptions were like the material itself: disorganized, confusing, hindered by a Superego injunction that had declared the matter unworthy. It was about peer discourse, in which I was a witnessing if not central figure. An exchange about frequency of analyst/analysand sessions had gotten heated and lost, had traveled regressively southbound, and had then ground to a muddy halt, with principals across divides lowering their eyes, poised to split off, give up, and head back to their respective silos to form separatist unions.**

How like the history of psychoanalysis that would be, actually—forged by years of secret-society-like meetings on a Wednesday night in Vienna over a hundred years ago. That's the legend. Back to the present day: groups had been talking recently; specifically, the group pool of candidates, which is a small subset of community members of an institute, had been talking, having been thrust together with an institutional charter: we are the future of instruction, of contact with the community, candidates had been told, of training and the message of psychoanalysis, which is . . . what? Inclusive! There's the word. Not the first word, certainly. Not the most important word, necessarily. Just one of the recent words, one of the important, recent words to add to our bandy lexicon. We need to be inclusive. We need to spread, that is, grow, as a movement, venture into the community, and above all dispel a prejudice that we comprise elitist, urban-centered, pluralistic yet racist elements within our midst. Actually, this isn't so new. Psychoanalysis has been treading this path of increased inclusion ever since it began. We know because we're candidates ourselves, and we've been told the rough history of inclusion and exclusion battles. We've been included, and we might not have been originally, because some of us—like myself—are not doctors.

Anyway, how do we do this inclusion thing? That was the group discussion, sort of. Actually, it was a system-wide, as in institutional, discussion, in the United States at least. We knew this because of something called the Holmes Commission on Racial Equality in American Psychoanalysis, which was established in August 2021 and completed its work in 2023. As a result, candidates and faculty were tasked with posing, informally and not, some long-incubated and now pressing social questions: How do we extend psychoanalysis to those who may still feel shut out, thinking that psychoanalysis is inaccessible for would-be patients or candidates? On behalf of the latter, some submit that the pursuit of inclusion entails the alteration of admissions procedures or training standards such that more will be enfolded into analytic training. Some hold that fewer personal analytic sessions per week for training candidates will create room for more patient care sessions in their practices, with fewer cases necessitating four-times-per-week analysis for their patients, as that standard is being reduced to three (or three to five) times per week, in keeping with an APsaA directive, which alters the criteria for analytic training to allow three-times-per-week frequency for control cases and training analyses. This will in turn cost those patients less money, and so candidates will be spending less time (okay, one day per week) in their own analyses, which in turn means they will be spending less money on training as a whole or having more space to earn income instead, and that will mean that would-be candidates with less time and resources for training, which by implication refers more to persons of color than white people, will have greater access to training in the first place. For would-be patients, something similar: we must make access easier, less expensive, geographically closer, or else render distance irrelevant by embracing telehealth. There, that's why this peripheral matter is important, because among other things numbers are important.

Whew! That all seems difficult to read, to write again, and to say again. It is uniquely fatiguing, this framing of the topic, from its details to its potential breadth, minus what is unknown. The details feel limp and repetitive, and limited, partly because they address only the known, concrete elements. They speak to the external, someone's analyst might further critique, adding that the external leaves out so much. It's a good thing we're not robots. Wait, will nonhumans be included somehow? Robots would do well with the numbers, be comfortable with just the numbers. It's interesting to think that some in the culture beyond psychoanalysis (and sometimes within) think that analysts act like robots. They're "blank slate" figures, watching their patients coldly, impassively, withdrawn with their protracted silences; they give autocratic, "top-down" interpretations that impose theory on patients rather than applying theory after diligently listening. "Why can't they be more human?" asks an anti-analytic trope. Maybe these critics think that AI will soon infiltrate the world of psychoanalysis (if it hasn't already), make us all redundant by the mid-21st century. Well, it's not likely. We can be complacent about some things, we think: that people want to talk with people; that they want listeners, thinkers, creatures with imagination, a more-than-academic take on the unconscious—possibly humor. Seriously. Yes, humor. The science of AI seems a ways off providing these qualities, so maybe analysts will be among the last to succumb in that dystopic fantasy. So far, robots can only do what's predictable, which is popular, actually, and this might mean that robots could ask scaling questions. "From 1 to 10, with 10 being the worst, how do you feel?" Ever answered a scaling question? I have. "Ten," I once kept saying, alongside expletives, wanting morphine for the kidney stone that was sliding down my groin. A robot of sorts appeared to listen but then acted, thankfully.

Pharmaceuticals can alleviate pain. Bots can help produce workbooks, self-help literature, or rote movie screenplays. Talk about humor: Hollywood never did right by psychoanalysis, most of us would say. In some ways, AI is quite old-fashioned. Only robots are still leaving me voicemails, for example. Anyway, if analysts are among the few left standing (or reclining comfortably in a black leather chair) in the mental health workforce, it would be a last laugh at those who moan about blank slates.

Thinking about numbers feels robotic. Staying on the surface with numbers is reductionist, both literally and theoretically: a place to start a conversation but also to end it, which feels like death, which is also robotic. Where is that conversation's life in between its beginning and end? And that's just in the writing of the idea. The talking is worse. As in the opening vignette, we speak of these topics in supervision, half aware that we are limiting our scope with questions about numbers, the "how many times" issue. Our supervisors and (especially) our training analysts agree; however, the former hold the notion that numbers, as in the number of sessions per week, does matter as an analytic issue. Regardless, we shortly turn away to that which feels more *alive*: verbatim process notes from patient sessions that expose what we choose to write down in order to expose ourselves to critical yet nurturing feedback. This is a feature of close one-on-one supervision, originally devised by onetime IPA and Berlin Society president Max Eitingon to teach pragmatic aspects of clinical treatment. Eitingon would have students take detailed notes on their sessions, which senior analysts would then review to detect and rectify mistakes. In keeping with this tradition, candidates take such notes today, though it's up to us what we share and what we edit out. Hiding, we capture the words of the patient more than we do our own, thinking that the crux of the exercise is to focus on *them*—that is, unless your bias is toward the relational, in which case the focus is on an in-between, a third, or a "field." Yet this is the business of analysis, and of supervision, this capturing of what indeed is happening in analysis between its players. It feels more human. And so supervision feels very human. The mood between candidate and supervisor is conversational, collegial, and for brief moments it's possible to feel equal to the supervisory figures who speak and sound like they have your back, but also your analytic future, in their hands, only they're nice enough not to say so very often. Power imbalances, like sex, are best left repressed.

Supervision and Candidate Standards

I make fun of Pedro for not paying enough attention to numbers when selecting supervisors—numbers, as in the numbers of years spent in training. But, having questioned his picking a supervisor who had not yet achieved the status of supervising analyst when they began working together, I will concede that if one is going to spend two or more years talking to someone (mostly) about one case, it better feel like a good fit. According to Tuckett, Junkers, and Zachrisson (2008), supervisors gather at conferences far and wide, sharing the work of their candidates, declaring the soundness of training yet fretting about the positions they hold, the power they have to fail a candidate or else sanction their progress toward graduation. Previously, Tuckett (2005) had put forth a three-frame model that describes the way analysts are conducting analyses: how they are engaged as an observer, how they apply conceptual background, and how they are intervening in sessions. Supervisors roundtable what qualities are necessary in order to be a psychoanalyst, observing that such evaluations are invariably subjective and therefore flawed. Nonetheless, they come up with lists of qualities for candidates to consider, framed by a prefacing question: Can candidates in analytic training . . .

- follow a flow in a session?
- establish contact with the unconscious?
- be modified by experience with a patient?
- tolerate ambiguity?
- utilize their training analysis and supervision?
- recover from loss of analytic stance?
- keep a "free floating attention"?

There's no humor included on that list, or whimsy—not explicitly. Nor are there extraneous factors that burden the candidate's training, unless worrying about money, time, being judged by faculty, and so on all fall under the "tolerate ambiguity" heading. That's ambiguous, we'd suggest. Not making procedures or policies clear—that's an actual complaint leveled by some candidates toward their training institutions. That's because the process isn't supposed to be that clear, faculty might reply. Anyway, can AI do any of those things on that list? It's a daunting list for humans, never mind robots, and surely difficult to keep in mind at any one time. A robot could recite the list. Of course, that's just a few of the criteria that analysts have come up with. There's plenty more, or there's more language that might convey roughly the same set of standards only with different word configurations. As to institutional matters, supervisors surely have views on the matters of inclusion, having once been included themselves. Maybe they were once in a category of outsider, whether professionally unqualified or lacking resources, feeling marginalized as people of color, perhaps, or as women. As insiders, they will have considered standards, thought about frequency of visits, estimated the income necessary to pursue training, plus other resources, like time. Views are sparingly offered, partly because our time is limited, though only in material reality. Otherwise, analysis takes forever. Training takes . . . well, not forever. But we move on. Time doesn't stop. It's like the unconscious—timeless. There isn't really an ending, so in a sense training doesn't end either.

That's a scary, vaguely immortal thought, so back to the logistics, the robotics that promise endings, which exist one way or another. Embedded in the list, in its subtext, is a capacity for endurance, framed as a numbers game, testing appetites for inconvenience, our tolerance of physical discomfort, our energy reserves, our discipline, our hearty vigor. If you're a candidate in analysis four times per week, and your training has straddled a pre- and now sort of post-COVID world, then you'd have four appointments per week around which you'd need a spare hour because you'd probably be traveling to and from that analyst's office on days that you work. And since most analysts who provide a training analysis seem to work only during business hours, this will more or less force your practice into nonbusiness hours, evenings, or weekends. Or not quite, you might think, unless you add that at some point in the future you'll have weekly supervision meetings with as many as three different supervisors, which will also require some traveling, plus the aforementioned gaps before and after these appointments, again during standard business hours; that is, unless you are still practicing (analysis and supervision) the COVID way[1] and therefore conducting some sessions by phone and possibly driving while listening, which may be a way to cut a corner or two and retain some semblance of sanity—sorry, normalcy. *Cut a corner.* Who does this? Seriously, who in their right, analyzed or not, mind would undertake this kind of routine if they'd really thought about it? Must be an unconscious choice to do something *that* difficult. Meanwhile, was that a corner you cut while you were listening hard to your patient as you plucked that ticket from the machine at the parking garage that one time? Was that analytic listening? And did you nearly strike that jaywalking pedestrian that other time, and moan that rules of engagement in modern society were breaking down.

Recent analytic training candidates may agree that COVID yielded a serendipitous gift of time: collectively, we spent more time at home, holed up indoors, mostly with family, learning the games that kids play with naturalized skill. People spent more time alone, not seeing friends, or attending gatherings, whether social or work related. As live contact became riskier, sex and romance seekers may have swiped left more readily, preferring to survive than to seek pleasure. More propitiously, we've spent less time in cars on freeways over the last four years, cutting corners in a rush to get somewhere. We have more time for the internet, to binge-watch sci-fi dramas that poach from history but set themselves in the future, predicting something dire, extrapolated from dire present-day scenarios—pandemics excepted. We have more time for video games with a new kind of storytelling, conducive to digitized minds and quickly flitting eyes. We dream and dread, diffusely, worriedly, of AI intrusion. We devote time to something less stimulant like reading, to listening, to everything psychical that attends psychoanalytic training. Many analytic readings engross us. Some are like lullabies. We've read them before. For some patients, COVID poleaxed jobs overnight, forced distressed date nights with a résumé. It literally pushed hairdressers and waiters onto sidewalks to do their jobs. It left much of our proletariat on the unemployment rolls, dawdling during business hours, more convalescent than rested as months or even a year or two went by. Thankfully for these people, evictions were forestalled, and something like therapy was needed for the depressive gaps in time, but those who wanted multiple sessions per week to explore the unconscious, whether life had turned upside down or not, seemed few and far between. The scarcity of patients wanting psychoanalysis isn't unique to the COVID era, and it's premature to say whether being forced to stay inside enabled people to *look inside*. Anyway, as candidates, we grab at patients who seem eager, available, and of course—one other thing now worth mentioning—who haven't died.

That's something of a guilty thought to commit to print, especially as thoughts turn to the future. Hope lives, for psychoanalysis, its patients, its analysts, and for its training candidates. Okay, so you're a candidate who is learning analysis, professionally and personally, while pursuing a living despite social obstacles, including public health and technological changes that are unprecedented. You reach benchmarks, eventually: you finish seminar, graduate, have a case approved, become accepted by the IPA, whatever. When do you arrive? When are you really an analyst? More importantly, when is an analysis really over, which is a wholly different question than, say, has a candidate done enough to cross the threshold of institutional acceptance? This is a waking dream, this rumination—quite a getting ahead of oneself, to be sure. We move back and forth, from the concrete or the trivial to the abstruse, wondering what conditions allow for an optimal analytic situation. The matter is dizzying. How important a matter is frequency of analytic sessions? We know it's not the most important thing in analysis. Analytic attitude: that's a thing, *the thing*, some would say. Maintaining analytic attitude means thinking analytically, interpreting consistently, says one of my supervisors. What's the right attitude of the patient? Being able to hear and engage with the analyst's interpretations and then demonstrating some manner of change in their lives. Why is four times per week necessary to help make this happen? We've heard one succinct, heuristic answer that suggests what is behind the numbers: it makes a difference when one is in analysis more days than not during any given week. Hmm—there's that ruminative sound again—that sounds cleverly axiomatic, and perhaps a bit simplistic, but if it's true, it's surely a phenomenological position born of a rough aggregate of experience.

Perhaps frequency of meetings is a matter of ritual with industrious overtones. Psychoanalysis is like one's job, something to work at several days per week, with weekends off. While it typically calls for a precise temporal frame, with each session a consistent length and measured down to the minute, it also dallies with a jazz-like profusion in which improvisation and flexibility are privileged. Sessions end when they end, says a Lacanian muse. Psychoanalysis dies because thinking has stopped or because energy has flatlined. Qualities of aliveness (something we want, apparently), rhythm, and continuity, or "going on being," as Winnicott put it, shape what is a malleable framework of treatment, not reified units of time. Despite his irreligious bent, Freud set a standard with a familiar ring by meeting with patients six days a week. Was Sunday his day of rest? Some think that an extra level of deepening is discernible from an intensive frequency of meetings. The transition from a life of minimal reflection to one aided by the presence of a near-daily listener has a plethora of effects: more continuity of reflection loosens associations, enables the working through of reminiscences that lead to suffering, says the Freudian. A dissenter might argue that repetition is mere addiction, that psychoanalysis is prescribing a perversion by its insistence on meeting so frequently and for so long, beyond decent levels of satiety. We might assert that what repeats and dies is more likely what happens in between sessions, where habit, psychical defense, reconsolidates. Deepening happens in the presence of another and in an internalization that endures and tolerates absence, even though conflicts emerge from those "breaks" between sessions: from the Winnicottian "breakdown" to the phenomenon that negative transference—hate—must be endured in treatment. This is the Kleinian bias, to not end the process before something unpleasant and thermal has been dealt with. Otherwise, psychoanalysis soberly resigns to fate, yielding to an amorphous, disappointed, or defeatist recognition that some experiences, feelings—drives, we might suggest—just do not alter meaningfully.

A History of Inclusion

At least it's good to know that psychoanalysis has thought about standards, whether they flex and move, dance to a rhythm, or lie still and fossilize. Imagine the training experiences of all those famous figures whom we can name-drop with ease to signify that we are in training and have listened well in all of our seminars. Or we took an encyclopedic interest in the biographies of Gay (1988) and Makari (2008) and derived from their biblical density the wide genogram of thinkers, leaders, and rebels. Think of the fledgling trainees of history, or at least of those post-1920 who later became standard-bearers of training institutions: people like Melanie Klein, D. W. Winnicott, Ronald Britton, Wilfred Bion. Klein

(1935, 1946, 1957) in particular altered the landscape of training. Interpreting fantasies and transferences of children as young as two or three, she argued that children suffered under a fierce and punitive conscience before an Oedipal phase of development (between three and five years old). She conceptualized the famous complex as resulting from early oral sadism that was partly constitutional and partly a reaction to frustrated weaning—not castration fears. For Klein and a generation of followers, the breast replaced the phallus as the nexus of development. The mind is organized by the relation of the self to its imaginary inner others, or objects, as they are termed. In early development, objects are partial, split into the all good and the all bad. They are the good breast that nourished and fed or the bad breast that frustrated the hungry child.

Klein's theories were contentious, placing her at odds most notably with Freud's daughter Anna. From the mid-1920s onward, the two feuded over theory and its application to child analysis in particular, though it was hardly the first major battle of the psychoanalytic project. Previously, women like Karen Horney (1924, 1926) had joined the movement, reexamining female sexuality and contesting the Freudian view that saw girls as little more than damaged little boys. Psychoanalysis doesn't appear to encourage heroes, but it may have needed its heroines, plus heroes to clear a path for them. Otherwise, idolatry is reticent and adherents seem to disdain the limelight that psychotherapy covets. Wilhelm Stekel, who conceived of Freud's Wednesday Psychological Society and who later advocated for Viennese psychoanalysts versus supposed usurpers from Zurich, gets mentioned in *Catcher in the Rye*. Not sure if that mainstreamed his fame. Anyway, few analysts become pop stars, so the psychoanalytic message to mainstream society is a dog whistle infused with myth, an esoteric lexicon—for many, a seemingly inaccessible ether of thought. Some early male principals of the analytic "project" were counterrevolutionary, separatist before analytic training was institutionalized, like Alfred Adler and Carl Jung. Both challenged libido theory, with Adler claiming that aggression and misogyny caused the repression of all things. According to Makari (2008), Jung was once a coy loyalist with respect to psychosexuality but later turned his attention to matters of mythology and astrology, much to Freud's dismay. Contrary to Freud, Jung praised religious rites, compared psychoanalysis to confession, called the earliest phase of life presexual, and came to believe that societal proscriptions against incest were not sexual but instead a defense against the desire to return to the womb—the inheritance of a matriarchal past, not a patriarchal history. History records that he and Freud split ways around 1913, with the former establishing a split-off psychoanalytic movement that bears his name instead.

Like Freud, Jung and Adler dealt with meaty matters, stuff of history as well as theory, plus the question of whether biological drives or something else is the primary driver of human will. And what about later outliers, Reich and Reik, who will have injected politics and socioeconomics into discussions of how psychoanalysis fits into the modern world? Wilhelm Reich weighed in about free clinics, free analysis, money, and time, and in so doing suggested a bridge between Freud and another revolutionary, Karl Marx. In the 1920s, Reich was a staunch supporter of the downtrodden, taking psychoanalysis and sex education to the streets, as it were. Traveling around Vienna, he provided workers with sex counseling, sexual hygiene, child counseling, and contraceptives. Beyond his activism, Reich was also influential as a leader of seminars, teaching students of psychoanalysis. He directed seminar leaders to discuss their failed cases and clinical errors, as Freud had done with the case of Ida Bauer, better known as Dora, some years earlier. He believed strongly that patients' defenses ought to be interpreted. Taking a "resistance first" stance, he insisted that clinicians should interpret the ways patients hold back their thoughts before interpreting what was being held back. Unfortunately, though politically informed, Reich appears to have been impolitic within the psychoanalytic establishment. Makari (2008) reports that by 1929 he was feuding with nearly everyone, thinking Freud was in error theorizing about a so-called death instinct. Freud in turn rebuked Reich, thinking the latter a fanatic for proselytizing the curative powers of orgasm.

Theodor Reik's story seems even more relevant to our issues of training, psychoanalytic education, and candidate inclusion. When did he start to believe he was an analyst, or that he would even merit training, for that matter? When he was being encouraged by Freud to dispense with medical school? That would do him no favors with some in the medical or then-burgeoning psychoanalytic establishments. Many believed that Reik was quacking his way through life as a lay analyst and cited the Vienna penal code to support their case against him. So he got some financial support from Freud along the way and later inspired one of Freud's papers on lay analysis. And he was not without his own ideas, weighing in on the matter of analyst silence, for instance. Silence as a regular part of the analytic frame conveys something to an analysand that more active interventions don't (Reik, 1948). Thanks Teddy, you paved the way on one front—on the question of who qualifies for training—and then offered thoughts on nonverbal communication that were likely ahead of their time. You are referential for all of us layfolk, and you took some shots on the chin, all so that we could access training and possibly become psychoanalysts today. You earned a mention in that lawsuit in 1988, the one leveled by the American Psychological Association against APsaA because the latter had been excluding all but physicians for analytic training for decades (the APA won). This isn't about equality. In the topical diversity, equity, and inclusion (DEI) debate, equality, as nuanced from equity, is absented. As a concept, it seems suspect: on the one hand, a vague term that for some confuses outcomes with circumstances and opportunity; on another, a refuge for those uncomfortable with Oedipal guilt or pre-Oedipal shame, the vicissitudes of feeling better or worse than others. So, equality aside, with the privilege of inclusion comes responsibility. Now we have to weigh in on some tricky, inclusion-oriented questions, like whether a four-times-per-week analysis is really necessary.

Idealization, Silence, and Analytic Freedom

This mooted institutional involvement may depend on how often a candidate pays attention to matters like continuity and change, not to mention where that leads in our own analyses and with our control cases. With continuity, certain phenomena, like idealization of the analyst, emerge first, we think (or are told), and this rarely seems like the onset of deepening. It's more like a recapitulation of an Oedipal event, marked by an abatement of resistance—a welcome, happy event, no doubt, but a thorny rose that should expose unconscious desire and lead to conflict. As a candidate, one starts to notice that a patient is eager for something from a treatment process but is ever inclined toward familiarity, which sets up expectations that fate will likely undermine. A patient who has been in analysis for years has become accustomed to frequency of visits and seems available for a different, unknown experience but is anxious about change. One day, a session begins late. The analyst opens the door to his office a minute later than usual, and in that minute the subject's anxiety betrays a dependency on familiar structure, furthered by an experience of an idealized analyst who can do no wrong. Had they (the subject) gotten the time wrong? Had the analyst canceled the session and the patient forgotten, or not listened to an instruction in a previous session? Had something awful happened to the analyst, hence that door remaining ominously closed? Just how important is this exercise that it needs to be attended to or even remembered? When the door opens, the subject breathes a sigh of relief, as it will seem then that none of the fantasies were true. But important questions arise: Where do those fantasies come from? Will the patient talk about this moment and what might be learned from it? This kind of event, trivial as it may seem, is the beginning of something different.

Originally, a subject may not have signed up for an analytic frequency of three or four times per week but be aware of an urgency or a desire for an undefined more that is analogous to our experience as candidates. That repeatedly invoked "more" may initially present in the face of a crisis, not so much a curiosity about feeling states that emerge from everyday occurrences that pass benignly, undigested as meaningful happenings. Elsewhere and previously, something has occurred that has left the patient desperate for more support, and in this state of mind they'll be asking at the end of the hour for another session should a cancellation occur. At this point, there is expectation that openings exist, that other patients come and go, take vacations, have sick days, or just don't need to speak some weeks, which the would-be analysand used to consider a pretext for their own cancellations. Something has changed. Now the crisis that spurred the treatment may subside or perhaps be enfolded into a broader impression of what treatment is or what it could become. Something about that "crisis" was illustrative of a larger, longer-term problem, this person considers. Or that problem itself has yielded to another desire, something the subject might cast as existential and exploratory, but not problem-solving in a conventional sense. As Pedro recently quipped, you enter treatment with a problem, but you leave with about 17. Before committing to a process that is concretely laid out (four times a week?), the subject may fight against the belief that such help seeking, once deemed necessary, may now seem expansive, an indulgent solipsism (aka navel-gazing), and possibly wasteful of time and money. The question of how important is it to know one's mind emerges.

Around this point in the process, the subject may also notice that a floundering, nonplussed state in which there is no known agenda for a session is not a reason to discontinue treatment or cancel a session. For some, this will have been a surprise, as they were prone to social withdrawal when at a loss for words, blank in their thoughts. This is when they hid, when they excused themselves, exiting stage left from potential exposures. They were conditioned loners once, daydreamers and drifters, or else obsessive, busy-life seekers. At times of stress, they may notice their states of mind and pause for thought, or they might not. They might get busy with tasks, putting solutions ahead of problems. Or they may let their minds wander and escape. Either way, it won't have occurred to them to let someone watch and wait, much less to pay for that kind of witnessing on a regular basis. Alone in the presence of another, Winnicott (1958) observed, speaking to this happening in an analytic space. Being watched while you think. Strange, an average opinion observes. Voyeuristic, a casual observer might opine. Winnicott used the phrase "capacity to be alone" to denote a state of being, of mind, not a literal state of aloneness. This being alone is a sign of tolerance of ambiguity, plus an integration of conflictual feelings, love and hate, illusion and disillusionment. In other words, he cast the ability to be alone as one of the most important signs of maturity. In treatment, a patient would have to feel this kind of moment, decide for themselves whether it feels salutary or perverse, and yet may not be able to articulate its value either way. At the point of observation and feeling, they may lack the words for description. They may be navigating one marker of analytic resistance: Are they in the room, allowing for their own spontaneity, relinquishing a plan for therapeutic action, yet present with an irreducible purpose? Will they allow the purpose to emerge the moment, in relationship with that largely silent, listening presence that is an analyst?

That task of being a listening presence is complicated by the demands of training. A candidate has a control case and is midway through a week of four sessions with a patient. Let's say the case is one year in, going well in a generalized sense, meaning the patient is cooperative, attending sessions regularly, being alone in the presence of the analyst, allowing that witnessing. But the candidate has a divided attention, listening on the one hand but also taking verbatim notes of the sessions so they might be examined in detail in supervision. This is usually a fruitful exercise, especially when the notes are accurate, because that allows for a supervisor to pause a consultation and make observations. There are moments in a session that can be isolated, highlighted. Supervisor and candidate can discuss the moment, consider factors of transference and countertransference, what was said by the patient and what that meant, and what might have been said by the candidate, either instead of or in addition to what transpired. In a good supervision, this discussion is respectful if by necessity critical. Parallel to a good analysis, a supervision doesn't just direct. It doesn't insist on an approach, Pedro asserts, or appeals—it's hard to tell sometimes. Case conferences, in which candidates present process notes to a cohort plus faculty, tend to be less critical, likely because of the group format. In that forum, group member associations, our reverie-like musings to material, are encouraged instead of comments that might be prescriptive or critical, plus a spirit of gratitude for the bravely presenting figure usually governs discussion. A reader might wonder if recordings of sessions are common in analytic supervision. They might be, as there doesn't appear to be standards on this matter—more like supervisor-plus-candidate preference. Compatibility: Pedro's standard, my idea of a bonus. Verbatim note-taking of sessions? That appears to be a norm if not quite a standard.

It's tempting to ask supervisors if they'll dispense with conventions like taking verbatim process notes for analytic cases, especially those that seem to transpire with imagination-stirring silences. For one thing, we can imagine different kinds of silence: hostile silences, awkward silences, silences that say, *I'm not going to answer that*. There are patient silences, compassionate silences, silences that get out of an analysand's way, saying in effect, *Don't stop, keep going, you're doing fine*; these are finessed lulls, not static gaps in a process. As candidate analysts in training, we'd be silent so as not to steal the initiative of patients. After all, sessions are their time to explore and at times demonstrate thinking, not for us to perform with precocious intrusions, what we may believe are our brilliant insights. Silence gets a bad rap outside of psychoanalysis, and even within psychoanalysis if it is clumsily used. The potential space it allows can deaden if left to drift. For some, such silences represent blankness, which can seem obtuse or uncaring. It is abandonment. In the context of social concern, silence now represents hiding and cowardice: not taking a stand on important matters of exclusion and inclusion, for example. Silence is linked to though is not tantamount to neutrality. It is Switzerland for an older generation with a European lens. Aloof and relaxed, it is like the Alps, lovely and *chill*. For a new generation that has a new bit between its teeth, neutrality is suspect. Silence is violence, says the zeitgeist. *We take sides*, writes a pop psychologist, like he's crafting a bumper sticker. Neutrality is something like whiteness, as that term is used by a vanguard of social justice activists—a still, colorless thing waiting for an unpleasant moment to pass.

Inadvertent silences amuse or irritate, like those brought about by Zoom incompetence. "You're on mute," we heard numerous times during seminar. In case conference, we'd be silent listening to another candidate present, waiting for our chance to say something interesting yet supportive. In supervision, we might flex downward our need to have verbatim notes versus, say, impressionistic, parenthetical thoughts about silences that reveal our countertransference responses. Take those patient (analysand) expressions about keeping busy with tasks, putting solutions ahead of problems, wandering and escaping. That's boring. Defenses are dull; they require an alert clinician to stay patient and endure. Listening is, for most of us it seems, more tiring than talking because listening entails more being with oneself *and* another. Anyway, whether a patient is interesting, entertaining, or stirring of our discomfort, a thorough capturing of session elements, spoken or not, is painstakingly hard. Taking notes in stenographic style while a patient is speaking, or as we think of what to say while poised to transcribe our own spoken thoughts, requires a level of mental gymnastics that by itself wearies the brain. It makes a spare hour after such a session, or a relatively frameless, didactic consultation with a once-per-week patient afterward, feel necessary. It either calls for or generates a degree of merger with the patient's mind, making more difficult the task of having an analytic thought, much less a thorough interpretation, because the task of concentrating on transcription is preoccupying. This divide between recording what's heard and having concurrent thought eases with experience. And yet not taking verbatim notes and therefore relying on memory for the postsession construction is also stressful and likely transfers much of the anxiety of an analytic hour to the hour of supervision. What creates more pressure: the task of taking verbatim notes during an hour, or the effort of recalling and transcribing them afterward? Or beyond that, of not taking any such notes and relying on memory, and perhaps imagination, when sitting with a supervisor who was not present at a session but seems able to place themselves in our analytic space? Indeed, at times it may seem as though the person listening to a representation of the analytic hour has a better vantage point than the person immersed in the hour itself.

Bion (1967) suggested that the latter strategy would help analysts listen better and therefore immerse themselves into a patient's experience. No memory or desire. This may feel true when the object that is the supervisor, their feedback plus all of the process notes from sessions, fades from consciousness, not disappearing so much as internalized, backgrounded. A feeling of relaxation, enlivening and prompting an alert motility, settles in. The noisome, itching feet and tickling nose become less distracting. The restless urge to get up and pace or else to slump down and sleep as though sleepless nights were a thing of the past is absent. Analysis, from the analyst's point of view, is enjoyable, freed up, like a candidate's first analytic appointment the day after graduation. Park that thought: graduation from full analytic training is a rainbow. Imagine that, we say, from our current place in the training pews, far from the box seats where the former graduates and now faculty sit. It could be worse. Some of us may recall a more archaic feeling, that of being under the influence of a foreign, nonpsychoanalytic institutional oversight that required not "process" notes but rather "progress" notes: summaries of practitioner interventions, plus patient responses that would signify (or not) their integration of standardized treatment goals. That was treatment reified in some preanalytic, before-time-like context where no one used words like *reify*. A world apart from the Bionian ethos.

Maroda (2022), for one, casts some skepticism on Bion's famous phrase, "no memory or desire": "I think it is not a realistic approach to doing treatment. I appreciate that his prescription was meant to encourage receptivity rather than deny our personal biases and needs. Nonetheless, his words are often taken literally, denying the considerable realities that prevent such a state from truly existing" (p. 10). It's true, Bion's caveat can be taken literally. Clinicians can infer that we don't have to take notes or refer back to them in preparation for a next session, as if continuity of process depended on such action. What if we were to come to each session with freshly open minds, not having done any homework—failing to recall, for example, when the patient asks, "Where did we leave off?" because they want someone else to hold continuity. For some candidates, this would stoke anxiety, make them feel unprepared, remembering times in school when they dreaded being called out in class because they hadn't completed the day's assignment. No doubt, some would have an opposite experience. They might interpret Bion's words as a relieving permission from one of our profession's esteemed elders. We can conjure Bion in late career, sunbathing in California, far from the austere, conformist quarters of London, saying to early career therapists and analysts, "Chill out. Don't work so hard. Don't worry about notes, the tiresome diction of the analyst-analysand exchange. Listen. *Feel*." Anyway, that's a caricature because yet another view is to suggest that what Bion was prescribing is actually harder to accomplish than anything previously recommended.

If the feeling of freedom, of spontaneity and aliveness, is the experience of the analysand during a mid- to late-stage analysis, or that of a candidate within an immersive stage of training, it might portend a termination: a finish line to both analysis and training. Gabbard and Ogden (2009) observed several criteria for an analytic ending, casting doubt on each one perhaps and suggesting that analysts spend much of their careers undoing what they learned in their training. And this sounds like a parallel to the Bionion ethos in which technique or theoretical orthodoxy yield to a less defined process. What a tantalizing prospect on the one hand, to undo learning. What a disturbing prospect on the other: wasted time, money, energy, and so on—similar to what may worry that trepidatious patient who is contemplating the commitment of analysis. What will it do to him? A candidate considers all those hours spent in class, supervision, training analysis, traveling between appointments, reading, absorbing, living a lifestyle of seminarian diligence—all so that they might let it go at some point and do their own thing? We conjure the happy, liberated figures, the former graduates whose rendered portraits may one day grace the walls of the center, ensconced in their offices, practicing with the "voice" that they birthed in training but developed more fully afterward.

But wait, did they get their hands dirty wiping down couches and doorknobs with cleansers in the sketchy post-COVID angst? Did they speak and listen live in their offices but behind actual (versus figurative) masks? As candidates today, we'll have missed out on or been spared some of the challenges posed by yesteryear's obstacles. But weren't our forebears spared the challenges of our pandemic-inflected era or the inconvenience born of calls for more racial diversity across systems? We realize that our emphasis on these present contexts might belabor a point that may seem obscure to future readers and later candidates in training. Perhaps it's because we don't want this moment in time, our unique moment of training, to be forgotten. Nothing feels more precious than the now that will be gone soon, even if certain artifacts, like telehealth, linger and expand in their use. Okay, so Skype and Zoom and Webex all existed prior to lockdowns, but their use has surely been kicked into the next gear by the COVID era. Now it's a rival totem to the couch. Now it's here to stay.

But what does it mean to have learned analysis, practiced analysis in the context of troubled times? Incidentally, if this thought were being shared in a seminar, the reader can be sure that someone in that seminar would feel bound to share an anecdote about D. W. Winnicott once alerting a roomful of colleagues to the reality of an air raid. That was the backdrop of London during the Blitz, of course. That was one yesteryear's example of an exceptional moment that defied formulaic thinking. Poor Winnicott—must be tough having people quote you all the time or retelling your folklore. Moving on to today and now beyond today's intersecting headlines: What does it mean to have an experience of analytic genitality, or having modified one's analytic Superego in order to provide what is a complete or near complete analytic experience? Do we simply exude the ability to love and work regardless of circumstances, the protean external? If a candidate crosses these broadly brushed thresholds, will it matter if they break tacit rules during or after training: caretaking for a patient who "acts out" with respect to fee paying, thus allowing an unwieldy balance to grow; indulging lengthy political diatribes of a patient without any pause for transferential interpretation? Or how about a weary day during which punctuality has lapsed and a session has started late and a patient hasn't seemed to notice? It's a free-thinking analyst's choice whether to take up the matter, make such a moment the substance of a session or some part of it. Or not.

In supervision, away from the daydream of analytic freedom, and long before the graduated release, a candidate seeks help in understanding a case, the nuanced moments in an analytic hour that are observable with supervisory distance. But we are also seeking approval. The stamp of support, an acknowledging comment, may arrive if a transferential current is spoken to by the candidate, if an underlying feeling of a patient, plus the defense that steered away from that feeling, is observed by the candidate and represented in their hurriedly written process notes, then heard by the overseeing mentor, who at times will leak out a satisfied utterance or even—dare we dream—a celebratory bray. The typical supervisor is flexible, we think, that is, patient and understanding of imprecision, the guesswork the candidate sometimes engages in as they stare at what they've transcribed, scrambling to make sense, give context for, explain, or even just determine the legibility of a written moment. As candidates, we hope these supervisors will regard us with Winnicottian care and think that our poor, disorganized notes are an expressive squiggle resulting from something our patients have projected onto us. We can be defensive of ourselves, of our patients, who may at times seem like defendants in a trial. Are they getting it, this analytic process? Are they freed up, associating with feeling, with a hold on memory? Or are they mired in those boring defenses, speaking in vagaries, trivial asides, lulling us and our yawning supervisors into flatlined consultations? We want to defend them just as they want to defend themselves. Is there really hate in the mind of a patient who is bleeding a session dry of life, in the heart of another who doth protest too much that they love their spouse and children but keep forgetting to do . . . whatever and flounders with confusion to match the defensively shoddy material?

The desire for achievement, growth, a finish line for the . . . patient(?) . . . may lead us in search of aha or bingo interpretations, those provided by a patient that would illustrate our good work and therefore deserved completion of an analytic control case. These are moments where the candidate analyst has made an interpretation and, perhaps because it has been given before, is at least a variation of what's previously been said (thus illustrative of analytic consistency). The patient appears to reflect back the interpretation with enthusiastic recognition and then adds their own inflection to an agreeable moment, suggesting their "voice" is coming to the fore, complementing the analysts that are us. They are like pet students reporting on their learning, recognizing the salient, nodal points of their analysis, demonstrating growth, winning *our* approval. When these moments occur, we feel a buzz of pleasure, like the pleasure a parent feels when a child wins a prize. It is as if we know the moments of success, so we scribble capably, for once capturing with unerring accuracy an illustrative process note. With luck or experience, we'll relax again, temper our excitable buzz, and recognize the need not to only postpone our pleasure but to qualify it, relay it to that object at the next level—the supervisor—who may likewise cheer as they hear of our winning moments. However, in this triangular arrangement, there is caution. The moment of apparent integration by the patient may not be what it seems. After all, depending on when these moments occur, there will be another session the day after, and the day after that, and so on. *We'll see*, candidates and supervisors are ever saying to one another. We'll need time and space still to determine whether the patient's self-analytic moment is a portent of analytic achievement or else closer to an early-to-middle-stage act of compliance.

So, as the months or even years of analytic cases pass by, candidates take stock of the analytic situation. We wonder if we're doing well enough, half encamped in the minds of our supervisors, imagining what they think, what they'll report to progressions committees or even say between one another given the casual rapport we project among them. Are they on our side, looking to shepherd us to places they inhabit, looking for the next generation to carry the psychoanalytic batons? Theoretically, we'd surely believe this was their goal. But are we good enough? we may wonder. Having been good enough to graduate from the smaller swimming pools, to enter "full" analytic training, are we good enough to finish it and thereafter join the guild? We blend these preoccupations with a desire to separate from evaluative gazes, which doesn't necessarily mean wondering for ourselves whether we are meeting program requirements. Childlike, we pause to consider whether we are "good enough" for ourselves, thinking or hoping that psychoanalysis is a bendy toy that we can shape to fit our own desires and neuroses. Relapsing away from abstruse or creative thought, we retreat from risky ledges into concreteness. It's an administrative numbers game, we'll remind ourselves, rewarding qualities of endurance and consistency, the happily knowable criteria. As we tabulate the sessions, observing them pass thresholds of two and three hundred over a two- to three-year period, we bring to mind the knowledge that Freud himself didn't have so many cases that stretched over years with such frequency of visits. That should bring further hope, then yet another reminder that psychoanalysis is not a numbers game.

indeed, that someone should once and for all write a critical essay on this topic titled "Psychoanalysis by Numbers" (if they haven't already).

"How many sessions have we had?" robots—sorry, candidates—ask. Had? Done? Performed? What do we even call the work when we're itemizing? It's like waking up from a stupor, this tired gaze at the spreadsheets that we submit for accounting by a training progressions committee. How much money have we made, and how much might we have made had we not lowered our fees to accommodate control case patients who balked at our hitherto hourly rates. That's opportunity cost, that missing revenue: something they don't talk about in training. It's too administrative, not analytic enough. That's for your accountants, the IRS, and your various debtors to listen to and contain. Don't want to get the hands and minds dirty counting the beans. It's not quite unanalytic to think in material terms while in training. It's more like it's beneath a bar of good taste: a whiny complaint that imputes guilt, betrays ingratitude. It's required, money, yet forgettable. Best not to think of all the money spent in training, in analysis. It will stagger the candidate, put pressure in the wrong place, give you bad dreams. Besides, "it," meaning your pleasure, which may require money, will come later, when you least expect it—certainly when you've stopped whining, stopped asking for it. Don't beg. Don't worry. Actually, don't even count. Learn to think of progress in qualitative terms, not quantitative. Think beyond numbers, or if you must, only count to three: that's the number of control cases you'll need. And the number two: that's the number of years you'll need for each case. And take it slow, enjoy the ride, and think of the precious now and at times the future, all of those analytic patients to come whom you'll treat for years and make a living from soon enough. The progress is slow when you're not counting the cost, but when you are it's downright glacial. You'll see. You'll learn.

Love, Hate, and Hiding

Learn, and then speak up for yourself when the time comes, when the cause moves you. Within institutions where a more direct advocacy of candidates occurs, such as speaking before a progressions panel and arguing for the merits of one's cases, candidates may wonder about other evaluative processes where candidates live (love?) and work separately from such discussions, relying on a chain of communication between faculty and supervisors rather than chances for an audience with their collective authority. In either situation, there is room to think about analytic achievement, to hope for experiences that may go beyond what is required for graduation. For example, is the necessity of navigating a negative transference, one laden with fear, envy, and hate and supposedly espoused by supervisors with a Kleinian orientation, actually required for achieving graduation? This may depend on the supervisors that candidates choose and for what reasons. If a candidate chooses a supervisor knowing that the person is Kleinian in their biases, shouldn't that candidate expect that this supervisor's approval of a case would be contingent on a satisfactory traversing of a negative transference, one largely characterized by aggressive desires? Or would a candidate, a novice analyst after all, be excused from having to know of and therefore accommodate such biases? Would institutions not expect those in a learning process to have *learnt* enough to have made such an informed choice in the first place? Consider what else would be apt in this situation: such a candidate might learn of other candidates' experiences, including those where a traversal of negative transference was neither required nor deemed necessary for a satisfactory analytic experience. Imagine the envy that this first candidate might feel, thus rounding out their experience of Kleinian supervision.

These Kleinian supervisors might expect candidates to recognize their negative countertransferences as well as navigate the negative projections of patients. Winnicottian supervisors might also emphasize this task, thinking the emotional burdens that analysts bear must also be examined. Winnicott himself offered an object lesson on this matter in his 1947 paper "Hate in the Countertransference." In it, he shared about a case in England, again during World War II, of a 9-year-old boy who lived at a hostel for evacuated children. The boy was a recalcitrant truant, at times in trouble with authority and often running away from something—not bombs, Winnicott insisted, but rather a neglectful and violent home life. Winnicott and his wife took the boy into their home, more or less adopting him while the analyst offered interpretations of the boy's drawings. Winnicott's treatment of him was disrupted by further running away and disruptive behavior, which aggravated the analyst. The boy was maddening—indeed, so maddening that Winnicott took to expelling the child from his home, after which the boy would have to appeal for a return. Ring the bell and you can come back inside, and we'll say nothing more about it, said the analyst, striking a bargain with the child. A time-out, of sorts. On one occasion, he explained this disciplining intervention, advising the boy that he'd been expelled because he'd made the analyst hate him. *Hate him*. Hate, like sexual instinct, is kept latent by awareness. Awareness prevents murder.

Beyond the analytic situation, are candidates meant to have negative transferences and countertransferences with their supervisors or further parallel conflicts with seminar instructors, personal analysts, peers, institutional hierarchy, or the broader culture of the analytic community? With all this talk and subtext of candidate neurosis relating to supervisory purpose, which may be autocratic in some cases or benevolently supportive in others, or something in between in most, where lies the evaluative gaze on the candidate's capacity for conflict? Of course, candidates apply to a training program, arriving with their own capacities for hate and their own baggage of distrust, inclined in some cases to regard authority as Cronos-like—driven to devour. And we have our various styles of coping with these feelings, ranging from pet-like compliance to reflexive defiance and niggling complaint, all of which we brought to the front door as fledglings. Maroda (2022) perceives passivity in many therapists who consult with her, adding that a reluctance to assert oneself stems from childhood experiences, having had no power over one's parents. But consider this: institutional culture also stokes those internal embers, this dialectic between the need to idealize and follow versus the drive to differentiate oneself. Indeed, the genesis of this very text was a paper that addressed a cross-institutional question fashioned by the IPA: what is the training candidate's experience of disappointment and disillusionment? That was the invited thought, the cross-cultural, international provocation: to consider how training had lived up to expectations or not. So the breadth of analytic thought and discussion on topics such as this is wide enough to allow disorder, to foster a paranoid state of mind in training, a potential breakdown. That may be an average experience. It really is, Holden would say, if he were a candidate. He'd have run away, probably, excluding himself. Anyway, it's not difficult to think that a hidden intelligence, inchoately machinated perhaps, has set the stage for a range of candidate experience that is rich with learning, which includes experiences that are collegial and friendly, but that ultimately calls for tolerance. Tolerance of psychotic anxiety.

So, by the time I was next talking to my supervisor, I'd changed my tune somewhat. On the surface, nothing was happening still. Beneath that, maybe a bit more. He pointed out, or suggested that I notice with him, that I seemed to have more questions than answers. It seemed like a criticism, and I was poised to ask him whether it was or not, but that would have been another question and so I held back, which means that my feelings answered my question. I replied, somewhat defensively—something I think I'm supposed to not be—that this was the way it was supposed to be: to have more questions than answers, not to stop having questions. He agreed, though not before adding that interpretation was still more important than questioning, in his opinion. Questions circumvent defenses. "You don't want to take more time than you need to, do you?" he asked.

By this point, I'd lost the context. Were we talking about the analyst-patient relationship or some institutional or worldly phenomena or all of the above? That's another question, I realized, and here's another: is it all intertwined? Meanwhile, my supervisor hadn't given up on dialogue. He likes me, I thought; actually, he's one of three that do. My analyst also likes me. I am immersed, so they're immersed with me, this cabal of mentors. And I'd like to think they all like me for some simple, uncomplicated, un-Orwellian reason, such as just liking me, as opposed

to liking me as a reaction formation against not liking me or what I represent. My supervisor, the first one I mentioned, followed up his question comment with some questions of his own: What's all this about numbers and logistics? Why was I making the matter of my training so much about such administrative details? These numbers are a distraction. Again, I was defensive, boring him perhaps. This is what everyone's talking about at the institution. It's all about numbers: numbers of cases, of sessions within cases; numbers of candidates across demographic categories; numbers as they relate to money, time. Well, my supervisor did with that what supervisors do, and what analysts do especially. They make it more personal, not accepting deflections to anything external. And so he delivered his interpretation, which I saw coming in the nanosecond before he spoke. I was more comfortable talking about numbers, about money even, than I was talking or thinking about internal experience. I nodded acquiescently. I actually did agree, even though I barely knew what he was saying. But then there was a curve, just a small one, but still something I hadn't thought of, and therefore had not yet learned. See, I hadn't yet weighed in, he observed. I hadn't yet said whether I prefer three sessions per week to four, much less five, or if I thought one or the other level of frequency was necessary. I didn't know, I replied. Truth is, I hadn't thought about it, like it was someone else's call—nothing to do with me. My supervisor then dove in for his tender, mediating kill: you've been hiding your opinions, he said. Then, finally, an unknowing speculation: "You might prefer three to four, with your patients or as a patient, because seeing an analyst more, wanting more, makes it harder and harder to hide."

Chapter 3
Style, Ethics, Ideas

It's a shame, this thing about a patient's words being better captured in process notes than those of the analyst. It's a shame because process notes would seem to be the best evidence for who we are as analysts, of how we're learning the process of analysis, evolving our analytic identities. This isn't necessarily true. Surely, we're on display in numerous other ways, in seminar classes, in supervision consultations—otherwise, in the in-between exchanges we have in other contexts. We're being ever watched, we think, as candidates. We're watching ourselves more than anyone else is, we imagine—a thought that is soothing. And not. We've heard a few people talk about this, one or two write down and publish the ideas. It's probably true that as candidates we learn more about what patients think than what analysts think. As many suggest, we should talk about countertransference more. It's also said that psychoanalysts and those who are candidates in analytic training don't like to do research. Or they don't want to do scientific research, so they don't weigh in on questions of treatment efficacy, for example, or deluge readers with survey-oriented research, as that follows only what people are aware of or choose to report. We're not in training to compete with the nonanalytic world. Wait, are we? We don't like to promote ourselves, our models of thought. We prefer the ethic and play of attraction, that patients will seek us out, not the reverse. Some of us like to write. Some don't want to write at all; they just want to talk or to listen. We don't really know. We haven't researched that idea either.

We all want to know what's on a patient's mind. We're committed to helping them, however we conceptualize the virtue of helping. That's what we're getting paid for, we think: to do what we think is *helpful*. We also want to put our best foot forward, show off our shiny new analytic skills, so when we present process notes in supervision or—better yet—in case conferences to faculty and fellow candidates, we transcribe our patients and ourselves wanting to know what's on our listeners' minds, and they in turn want to know what our patients think and said, but also what's on our minds, what we thought and what we said, because that process is about *our* minds. They (our fellow candidates) want to know how we felt, what our countertransference was, how it might resonate with theirs as they listen to the process notes—whether they would have thought and said the same things that we said and thought. There are some things they won't know unless we explain them: how we might have paused before delivering the best bits of our interventions. You know, that punchy, end-of-thought flourish, that trailing sentence clause that wrapped up nicely what you had to say before leaving space for the patient. The listeners want to know what's on the presenter's mind so they can learn, so they can compare, judge, envy style, the sheer taste of the analysis. That's a side of analysis that doesn't get talked about much: the aesthetics, or the feel. With all of the embodied senses that we privilege, where are they, these senses of taste, touch, and style? Where is the individual amid the orthodoxy?

The plight of the individual in training skims from the matter of inclusion to the opportunities born of exclusion. As Philips writes (2024, p. 81), being left out of something begins as a tragedy, and tragedy, Freud suggests, is integral to development. Freud, like Kafka, was concerned with exclusion. As irreligious Jews in Europe, they both fell into paradoxical positions, insisting that feeling left out is a human problem and that no one is excluded from the experience of being left out. Perhaps this is why inclusion as an antidote seems so important to us. We are frightened by and compelled by the phenomenon: some of our favorite historical or literary figures are beset with exclusion. I like Holden Caulfield. Freud was fascinated by Hamlet, by his displays of indecision, of uncertainty and deferral. Another of Freud's favorite books was *Paradise Lost*, also about a character who is left out. Philips observes that Satan's exclusions bring about the worst in him (no kidding) but adds that left-outness, as he puts it, brings solitude, which in turn makes something else possible. Exclusion becomes a medium for self-recognition, a learning experience that will later pay dividends. What one does with it is what counts, and so we have a choice upon being left out, about how we take ourselves to be, who we want to be.

Because of this paradoxical need to be alien, we'd fashion in our learning process a style that is necessarily independent from any set of rules. We'd choose a virtue and go with it, whether it was a manner of expression, a stance of distance or of intimacy. Brevity, for example, is deemed the soul of . . . something, possibly psychoanalysis, since soul is the meaning of psyche, and as Bettelheim (1982) wrote, imbuing psychoanalysis with a quality of soul was Freud's ultimate purpose, despite his early emphasis on scientific inquiry. As candidates, we are the inheritors of that purpose, plus that of Freud's now disparate offspring, many of whom disagreed with him and with one another: hence the diversification of contemporary psychoanalytic training. We think the are traces of either side of Freud's positivist/hermeneutic split in our own learning curves: We look to investigate a patient's symptoms and to enjoin patients in that in-depth search. At the same time, we remind them and ourselves that the task is gradual and complicated by the idea that our cooperative search is not just about eradicating symptoms or, within that task, of eliciting forgotten memories. The task of analysis is wrapped up in a notion of finding something elusive, and this something is similar to the notion of soul searching: settling on an idea of "I" that is personal but not pejoratively reduced (ego), we look for a total or whole self, one that is disguised by selves that are pejoratively termed—ego or false self—but which nonetheless represents our emotional and immaterial essences, that which connects us beyond a rational existence. And so we look to art, to play, to humor, and we do so in a manner that connects thoughts that connect the rational and the irrational in loose associations bound by strange needs, such as the need to be brief.

Less is more, says a seasoned analyst, a supervisor, regarding a passage of intervention read aloud by a candidate. You learn this with experience, she adds, meaning an analyst learns to coalesce material, pick ideas from the weeds, and at times craft a statement that speaks to the patient's mind, but an analyst doesn't overstate or complicate a thought. This recalls text from Meltzer (1978) in which the author marvels at Freud's treatment of the Rat Man (ne Ernst Lanzer), drawn from an archive of notes about that famous case that were preserved by James Strachey. "Freud's genius: that he could allow so much information to enter his mind and allow it gradually, very gradually, to become organized" (Meltzer, 1978, p. 56). Meltzer was struck by Freud's capacity to integrate detail into a phenomenological impression, to recognize character structure, his patient's identification with his mother, and Freud's capacity for nonjudgment with respect to the unlikable, obsessive patient. Others, like Kanzer (1980) and Mahony (1986), working from *Freud's Technique Papers* (Ellman, 1991), were less impressed with Freud's interventions, at least, thinking him too prone to suggestion still, plus argumentativeness, that Freud had not yet mastered the technical requirements for encouraging free association. At this point in his career, 1905–1910 roughly, Freud was like a candidate in training: still enamored of scientific rigor as taught by his mentors and not yet the analyst/philosopher of his later career. He drove into the Rat Man his idea of the fundamental rule of psychoanalysis. He made his patient pledge to say everything that came into his head, even if it was unpleasant. He added that he could not, as the patient's analyst, grant the patient the right to withhold a train of thought. That was beyond his power, he suggested, revealing a belief in some higher authority, in nature perhaps.

Whether or not Freud acted like an impetuous fledgling, the Rat Man appears have been a cooperative patient, at least telling Freud about his obsessions, which included a fear of a horrible corporal punishment involving rats being poured from a pot into a criminal's anus. Although the nightmarish images had not arisen from the patient's dreams or obsessions initially—rather, from the account of a military officer—Freud interpreted the rat horror as corresponding to a pleasure of the subject's own of which he himself was unaware. The patient responded more or less agreeably, revealing a fleeting thought about the rat punishment happening to someone dear to him. Upon Freud's prompting, the patient further revealed that the person to whom this "idea" of his related was a lady whom he admired. The Rat Man's disclosures did not come about easily; indeed, his resistance was such that Freud would have to remind him of his treatment's fundamental rule. Or Freud would be called on to sift through confusing, meandering material in order to make sense of the patient's obsessions—what appears to have impressed Meltzer. An example of this occurred when the Rat Man lost his pince-nez (glasses) and attempted to pay a debt that he felt he had incurred as a result of receiving a package containing his recovered glasses. In his notes, Freud admits to being confused by the Rat Man's contradictory accounts, but in a later session the patient chooses to reveal an important piece of personal information that had previously "tormented" him. He recounts with detail the story of his father dying of emphysema nine years earlier, and although the patient had sat with his father in vigil, the patient was asleep when his father died. For this he had reprimanded himself.

From accounts like this, Freud conceptualizes what neurotic obsessives like the Rat Man attempt with respect to self-reproaches. What the layman thinks, and would still think today, is that the guilt indicated by an obsessed-upon occasion—in this case, the instance of falling asleep at his father's deathbed—is too great for the occasion. It feels exaggerated. But the analytic physician (or not physician) says the affect of guilt is justified, even though it belongs to some unknown content. In session, the patient asked why the discovered sense of guilt had any therapeutic value. Freud replied that it was not the information in itself that had the therapeutic effect; rather, the unknown content to which the affect is attached is to be searched for and further understood. The guilt was the Rat Man's creation, Freud was saying. Self-reproaches can only arise from a breach of one's own moral principles; otherwise, we are moved to rebel and to regard ourselves as heroes. The Rat Man admitted that while he thought himself a moral person, motivated by guilt and prone to fantasies of punishment, he had done things in childhood that had come from an evil self that was now unconscious but in need of assimilation into an organized whole self alongside his conscious view of himself as a not guilty figure. Freud was saying he, the Rat Man, was a guilty person—guilty of something—or else why all the obsessions? This would be disturbing information for the Rat Man, who would not have readily understood the therapeutic task of reconciling conflict. It's interesting to note that from the record of notes, Freud said a word or two about the good opinion he had formed of his patient, which appeared to please the Rat Man amid his disrupted state.

A hundred or so years later, a man who has been in treatment about as long as the Rat Man (less than a year anyway) says that he wishes to end sessions. He believes he has achieved what he hoped to achieve in treatment: his insomnia has abated. Gone are his bad dreams, his daytime restlessness, his irritability followed by bouts of torpor. He has lacked motivation, he claimed initially. But now things are looking up. Besides the abatement of symptoms, his previously stalled and now late-stage career has been revitalized, though whether this is due to external factors like a bump in the economy is unclear. He and his wife are getting along better, and while the matter of his granddaughter's accusations of sexual abuse aimed at the patient are not resolved, neither have they expanded into a legal problem for the elder couple, as was previously feared. The thing is that nothing has been denied officially, despite requisite reports having been made to appropriate authorities, and within treatment itself the patient has intimated at least the general truth of his granddaughter's claims. But what's the point of delving into that now, he believes. What value is there in dwelling on the past? Besides, it was mostly a misunderstanding what happened. In session, he thanks me, his clinician, and issues an unsatisfying compliment: "You have been very professional," by which he means that treatment has avoided undue emotion and irrational action, not compelled distressing associations or made interpretations that might have exposed unconscious wishes, forbidden acts, and guilt. The style of the sessions had been uncoercive, and beyond that good-humored, even playful. "I've enjoyed talking to you," the patient concludes. I do not challenge this happy ending.

What a phony bastard, Holden would say of the patient, and maybe the analyst too. Doesn't want to get into it, the "it" being something that touches on our protagonist's known sensitivities: the plight of at-risk children. Holden would indeed be indignant about the alleged abuser and then wonder about the analyst's ethics in treating him. What would or wouldn't that analyst do to that patient? Why wouldn't the analyst go into it, as he'd put it—as he'd put it regarding himself and his own trauma-avoidant habits, he might notice. At this point our adolescent hero might still his own judgment and notice that scary psychoanalysts, those shadowy figures to whom he'd projected sinister, penetrating intent in the context of his own fiction, might be as wary of truth as anyone else. Why else would a professional behave like a "professional" and just let go of the most difficult aspects of a treatment? Why would that treatment stop just because the presenting symptoms, the most superficial elements of a pathology, which betray an unconscious guilt but couldn't ever yield a satisfying treatment outcome by themselves, had stopped. Had they stopped because an external threat had subsided, and did that mean anxiety or guilt had subsided also? And why would that mean that the work, the thinking, the feeling about what's internal, not to mention what's right and just, come to an end?

It would be no time for aesthetics unless an aesthetic element somehow served truth. This was Holden's complaint about aesthetics: it's phony. Movies are phony, he thought, which is why we'll ever have to imagine Holden because his author/alter ego decreed that no such depiction would ever be made of him. That renders him a deeper projection of ours, someone we can cast ourselves as. So, if Holden's spirit is in the room when something untruthful is going down, then something needs to be said, because unlike him we can't just run away. It would be a time for numerous treatment considerations to coalesce. Facing a premature treatment ending especially, an analyst would need to summon the ethic of helping or "doing no harm," to conceptualize insights as to why the patient was avoiding a furthering of treatment and why at the time of such an announcement in particular. An analyst needs to think about what to think, about what to say, about what's being said in a session, and about what's being left out. About the first category, the brevity of dark humor might provoke awareness and pave the way for a more sobering statement. Many a true word and so on. About the expression, "I've enjoyed talking to you," which is likely a defensive pleasantry, an analyst might reply, "I'm afraid I haven't, and perhaps we might revisit why you'd use that concept—enjoyment—to describe what has been a serious ongoing discussion."

A reason that patient might have enjoyed his treatment experience, or merely enjoyed his treatment, as if it hadn't contained any elements that were disturbing, may result from contemporary notions of therapeutic alliance. This bears the influence of figures like Kohut (1971, 1977), who attempted to demonstrate degrees of empathic attunement with patients and as a result emphasized mirroring statements in interventions rather than interpretations that might disturb a patient's unconscious, thus disrupting defenses that are habitual. A candidate in early training, or in training prior to analytic candidacy, learns to reflect patients' remarks back to them, thereby offering an acceptance of patients' experiences. But this wasn't the strategy of Freud in treating a case like the Rat Man, and it hasn't been the basis of therapeutic alliances in our training experiences, necessarily. We bring to mind cases of patients who exhibit pervasive patterns of defense, like manic or obsessive tendencies, repetitive actions. We hear in them repeated illustrations of Superego resistance ("I'm so stupid, unworthy") to replace thinking about problems; they act out thoughts and feelings, exhibiting what Freud observed in "Remembering, Repeating, and Working Through" (1914); they exhibit displacement, speaking of minor agitations versus major stressors, thereby diluting their focus and becoming confused. Or, they give brief voice to painful yet true thoughts only to undo their own insights with immediate follow-up thoughts and behaviors. Freudian theory teaches that guilt is the root of this reactive defense, and contemporary analysts like Maroda (2022) extend the theory to countertransference, observing that therapists and analysts pursue their careers looking to help people as a reaction formation against guilt.

Helping and truth seeking: a pair of categorical imperatives. Early in our careers, we were impressed with Kantian virtues, apparent categorical imperatives like seeking truth, helping people, broadly aware that these matters were complicated, though we tried to keep it simple. Keep it simple. That was the ethos in drug treatment programs, hospital-based care. Know what destructive behaviors are, know what defensive rationalizations are, then confront them in a straightforward, vaguely manful fashion. Be patient, compassionate if you like, if you must, but don't "mirror" defenses. That furthers their strength, keeps them embedded, hidden. Don't hide from the hidden. That is, don't let your interventions collude with those of the patient. That was the ethos in such programs, roughly paraphrased. Did the principals of those programs think that psychoanalysis was incompatible, unsympathetic to the cause? Well, they might have if they thought the method dominated by mirroring statements, misplaced empathy, or an indulgent drop into dreams, not material reality, that it gave attention to esoteric, Oedipal fantasies versus "real" attachment difficulties, broken parenting that is actually remembered.

Amid candidacy and beyond, those in psychoanalytic training are sometimes called on to venture into the community outside of our institutes: we host "forums" in the basements of local psychiatric hospitals where we present analytic cases inflected with analytic ideas; we teach courses within short-term satellite programs that branch away from our institutional centers. These are small classes, seminars, comprising mental health professionals working in a diffuse system of mental health care. They are interested in the dinosaur that is psychoanalysis, poking their noses into one of its offerings, these baby pools that sometimes lead to the level of full analytic training. And we, the candidates within that level, become one of those volunteers climbing the tree of faculty, cutting our teeth as pedagogues as well as analysts. We start talking to early career professionals or midcareer professionals seeking a change, about ideas of helping and truth seeking, plus the method of eliciting the unconscious. We'll share about the judicious use of interpretation—that primary method of intervention, as recommended by Freud—versus our use of silence, for example, or reverie, as Bion (1967) espoused. Meaning, we'll listen, speak of thinking, of thinking with the patient, inviting them into a co-constructing or cooperative-versus-authoritative exercise.

We come to believe that psychoanalysis is and has been informative of alternative treatment methods all along. It is more compatible with other approaches than is commonly supposed and has been for over a hundred years. In discussions with other professionals, presumptively nonanalytic thinkers, we observe tensions around what is helpful or what is truthful that are similar to our own. We recognize in ourselves the desire to empathize with a patient, to listen to and absorb their experiences. We feel the same need as any self-conscious helper does to be patient, compassionate, and kind. At the same time, we think that what is helpful is an acute observation of conflict in a patient's mind, minus a decision that would falsely resolve it. We think this problem is a conflict between conscious and unconscious, between desires, feeling states—what nonanalytic thinkers are calling explicit and implicit states, as informed by neuroscience. A patient presents a problem. They are angry with their partner, their boss, or their child. Someone doesn't get them, hates them. They think this is their trauma—the only trauma they're aware of as they think and speak. We listen patiently, holding in our minds that this isn't true, that something deeper, unknown, more complicated and yet once simple, is true. Do we declare what this truth is? Is the patient ready for that? We don't know, but we don't think so, so we tread carefully, thinking that the unconscious will reveal itself in sessions, in bits and pieces of action, in dreams, in the seemingly disconnected thought that comprises free association.

In a study group of would-be analytic candidates, I share notes from sessions to illustrate unconscious process. An earnest young man, seriously concerned with doing "in-depth work," begins a session talking about rock climbing. He soon chides himself for wasting time in treatment, but prompted by my judgment-stilling curiosity, he later observes a metaphorical link between his rock-climbing anecdote and later material. Nothing he thinks is irrelevant, he considers. In another session, another young man speaks brokenly about family dysfunction, his estrangement from a father and brother. He is torn between feelings of obligation and desires to turn away, escape with escapist behavior. This impression takes shape as he speaks uncertainly of his family "sticking together"—a Superego defense against his previous thought, a disparaging remark about his father's "manipulative" tendencies. Thoughts stick together, albeit tenuously, as in a stream as he reveals a repetition of his father's legacy. At a recent Christmas gathering, he ruined a chance to bond with his girlfriend, instead texting with flirtatious other women.

We believe there is a trauma before the so-called trauma that is consciously presented to us. That's an old idea. We think the latter-day or day-to-day problem is a displacement, a reenactment, the debris of a phenomenon that plays out in the treatment: transference, projective identification, afterwardness. These are the terms we've learned and may also disseminate; this is the language that has organized some thought of ours, helped us locate our experience, made some sense of it. We've had a felt experience of these insights, of our memories, and it seems to us that what we learn we will have known before. These felt experiences, "memories," aren't necessarily actual events. Nor are they fabrications. Freud describes fantasy as the mental representative of the drive: "an instinct can never become the object of consciousness, only the idea that represents the instinct can" (1915, p. 177). For Klein and her followers, unconscious phantasy, those paranoid-schizoid states, oral and anal sadistic impulses, are the representatives of the instinctual drives. This is the psychic drawn from the somatic. Giovacchini (1969, 1972) drew on Freud's concept of day residue in dreams, which refer to seeming insignificant impressions from the real world that are linked to infantile aggressive or sexual wishes. Giovacchini extended this observation to the clinical setting and thus made linking interpretations connecting spontaneous and seemingly irrelevant perceptions with unconscious process. Some will think this a biochemical phenomenon. Latter-day neuroscientists, such as LeDoux (1996), locate emotion and memory in the brain, and specifically in the temporal lobe, in organs that mediate emotional experience, promoting safety and survival in the unconscious, but calling the latter implicit emotional memory, not a dynamic unconscious.

This research has implications for treatment strategies, for it makes a difference whether one thinks of early experience as encoded within parts of the brain that are not responsible for autobiographical memory. If experience is not represented by words or images, then the aim of psychoanalysis becomes something different than the interpretation of unconscious fantasy that is repressed but accessible; rather, it becomes a process in which change occurs in the context of a relationship with the analyst, which suggests murkier therapeutic efforts composed more of gesture and action. In the vignette, the first figure, the rock climber, has something like an aha moment. He makes links, thinks of the layered meaning of his words, his interests. "Climbing!" he exclaims. He is ready for the insights that he may build on and use to alter his life, and my "style"—my attention to words, which includes quips and slips, plus the highlighting of their relevance—will help him think. He'll resume his climb, I believe. In the second case, the incessantly sexting, acting-out man seems lost in escapist behavior and projective fantasy. He is stuck, and his thoughts tenuously stick together; there is little, if any, integration. What will hold him together, keep him safe, keep his feelings contained? It's not clear, but it seems that insight born of words, images, memory, is elusive. He may not have memory at all as we commonly understand it. He doesn't know what to do; he barely knows what to think. Is he helpless? And if so, will he externalize with further projective defenses that he'll bring to the analytic space? Does he need therapeutic action that will direct him, point out the baby steps he needs to take so that he can resume his climb?

Guilt and shame: Where are they located in the brain? Does it matter? We might dismissively ask this question, thinking the issue nonchemical. Besides the neural geography, they seem like two feeling states that are in conflict, though they are sometimes presented as if they were interchangeable: "resistance was commonly due to unbearable guilt and shame over ambivalent ties to loved ones, as well as sexual desires" (Maroda, 2022, p. 90). The author is referring to Freudian assumptions: that innate drives toward sex and aggression are at odds with the environment as well as internal values. Resistance in treatment results from repeatedly pushing out of awareness disturbing thoughts and feelings. We may find this habit in a patient who seems inhibited and as a result appears to subdue desires, pull back thoughts and actions that may be desirable because of anxieties that emerge. Freud assigned this tendency to inhibit to castration fears, which seems anachronistic and sexist unless we stretch our imaginations and consider a broadened application of the metaphor: people subdue their assertiveness, including their desires, fearing severe punishment. The resulting symptom is depression, which manifests as a flat, deadened presence in an analytic treatment—the price of feeling safe from harm. Now, when asked about the meaning of this inhibition, a patient may speak of low self-esteem, of feeling inadequate to a task, rather than, say, preemptively guilty about asserting themselves, doing some harm and then facing punishment. This person may indeed struggle with unconscious guilt about desires and therefore subdue them as a reaction formation. Or a patient may struggle with underlying guilt about desire and displace anger onto lesser stressors, the noisome behaviors of others. The following case illustrates the neurotic confusion that can result when guilt and anger collide:

Dan is irritated because his wife's recent fall down a staircase and resultant injury has thwarted plans for early retirement traveling. He finds himself in a daily caretaking role, waiting on his wife's day-to-day needs while foreign adventures are indefinitely postponed. He is resentful, bitter even, yet guilt-ridden because this same wife has sacrificed so much for him, shown admirable forbearance after he'd irreparably damaged his career with a drinking problem, which once placed the couple in debt and near bankruptcy. She also stood by him when their eldest daughter turned on them and left home, accusing Dan in particular of verbally abusive treatment. Humbled and grateful, he entered treatment extolling his wife's virtues. Accidents happen, he says of her recent carelessness. But he can't help being angry with her for not taking sufficient care of herself and for being reckless on those slippery stairs.

But another kind of patient comes to mind who is less guilt-ridden, more shamefaced. Addicts and so-called narcissists seem to fit the following description: they do not so much inhibit their desires as act on them repeatedly, excessively. Then they feel guilty afterward, especially if they are exposed as having behaved in a way that runs afoul of Superego rules. They feel terrible, as in guilty, about having behaved badly, or at least about being caught behaving badly. Being caught with your pants down: that's the expression that also comes to mind. Examine it closely and it further brings to mind the idea of genital inadequacy, the theories of organ inferiority that Adler (1917) once proposed, apparently at odds with Freudian theories of instinctual drives and unconscious guilt. Shame, which is born of inadequacy, of feelings of unworthiness, seems a different animal from guilt, not a roughly synonymous state of mind. For patients, it seems like a precursor to guilt, a state of weakness disguised by acts of aggressive drive that in turn generates guilt. We have observed this in patients who present for treatment in the wake of acting-out behaviors that are destructive in relationships. In treatment, especially in opening stages, the emphasis in these patients' disclosures is on the harm they have perpetrated, the "trauma" they have induced in loved ones. When asked about initial motivation for the acting out that stirred the guilty feelings, these characters seem bereft of understanding. Instead, they are theoretically judgmental ("I have entitlement issues"), are haplessly apologetic, promising of better behavior, but usually hopeful (and expectant) of redemption as granted by someone else.

Using our analytic thinking, we can conceive of these patients' actions, plus the absence of reflective thought that is attached to them, as a varied defense against underlying shame. Within the acting out/feeling guilty cycle, we can observe a pattern of displacement: feelings of shame for being weak are displaced by feelings of guilt, which pertain to and result in doing harm but also in feeling powerful. Guilt is, in effect, a default position, chosen unconsciously over shame. Grandiosity displaces inferiority; feeling big undoes feeling small. We'll play the villain rather than the fool. Then this same denied feeling (shame of being weak) is split off, projected onto another, such as a loved one, who in turn identifies with that feeling of being weak and unimportant; thus, a generalized feeling of victimization results in them. Projective identification. Third, this is all a repetition of something from an acting-out patient's past, leading to repetitive enactment with loved ones that ultimately destroys relationships. Repetition compulsion. Mastery of trauma, Freud (1920) observed of this phenomenon. A child finds pleasure in repetitive play but also in the experience of novelty. Or they are unconsciously driven toward self-reproach, the punishments that either accompany or follow the achievement of pleasure. Does the patient who is acting unconsciously want something else than a return of the repressed? They won't achieve that genuine versus transient relief unless someone is alert to what is happening under the surface of not only actions but also pat, go-to answers. Unless an analyst has a framework for thinking about how patients turn away from disturbing thoughts and feelings by acting unconsciously, the destructive behavior, plus the analyst's unconscious identifications with those projections, will simply recycle, and little progress in treatment will be made.

In a session, Cindy spoke of feeling restless, uncomfortable. She didn't like feeling "needy" she said, yet she felt needy of family and friends. She needed family help with pragmatic tasks, with money. She needed attention from her partner, and was frustrated when her partner was unavailable, or was available but insufficiently engaged. However, she'd reverse her feeling in response to these stressors, especially with her intimate partner, whom she'd then describe as poorly organized and immature, losing Cindy's interest rather than the reverse. "I feel like her babysitter." Speaking past whether this was true or not, I observed that her view of her partner as a baby (by implication) served to subdue or possibly undo the feelings of neediness, of smallness and unimportance, that she'd previously reported about herself. Then she'd project these feelings onto another, in effect putting them out of her mind.

Of course, these conceptions and illustrations may also paint a simplistic picture. One candidate's learning curve may be another's obstacle after all. For some who have repeatedly gotten stuck with patients by not addressing problems, circumventing defenses, encouraging so-called positive behaviors but with little effect, or straining to mirror affects from displacements, learning an analytic approach has kept focus on patient problems without assuming responsibility for them. In learning a new approach, we haven't spared ourselves difficulties, but we have ways to think about and navigate feeling bullied or lied to by addicts and narcissists, for example. Or we can think about how we are manipulated by "needy" patients into waiving fees linked to absences or taking calls after hours because of professed crises that turn out to be nothing close to emergencies. Conversely, relational psychoanalysts might opine that some candidates will learn to be less rigid in their practices. We will look beyond strict adherence to rules, split dichotomies of correct versus incorrect technique, right or wrong therapeutic action, in order to provide an optimal nurturing environment. They'd likely offer that our strength as analysts ultimately lies in our capacities to be flexible, spontaneous, and creative. Little progress? They'd chidingly rebuke a previous thought in this chapter. Growth is an unknown, elusive, but ever-thought-provoking third point on an invisible triangle.

In a sense, I was lucky with Naomi, a bullish 16-year-old whose parents brought her to me shortly after the COVID lockdown. To be precise, they sent her to her room (a commonplace occurrence) wherein she'd have a late afternoon appointment with me—in theory, a break from homework time. Over numerous sessions, Naomi was anything but bullish with me over Zoom calls, which belied the reputation assigned to her. However, she was seductive. Laying on her bed, she'd position her laptop at the base and gaze into the camera, looming over me. Cooperating, she was awkwardly polite if distractible and often spoke in bursts, revealing thoughts that came to her in instants that she couldn't contain. Often, she spoke of her schoolwork, wanting my opinion on literary assignments especially. She'd heard of *Catcher in the Rye* but didn't know Holden Caulfield, she confessed. The character I subsequently described sounded cool, she said. She was into *Hamlet* instead because Denmark seemed like a prison like her home seemed like a prison. She was also prone to depressive insights and said she liked the bit with the prince and the skull, thinking it meant that it doesn't matter what we do and say in this life; it all leads to the same thing anyway. She'd sigh at moments like this and deny anger. "I don't care," she'd pronounce. Her other frequent expression was "I'm sorry," usually offered because she'd be late to sessions or sometimes forget them entirely. I started interpreting that aggression lay beneath these habits—an observation she'd deny with a thinly concealed sulk. Indeed, she was in the midst of such a denial one day when the door behind her opened, revealing a face illusorily cleaved by the narrow opening. Apparently, this was happening repeatedly, which Naomi explained when later justifying what happened next: "GO AWAY, I'M IN THERAPY, GAWD!" she bawled at her younger sister. Immediately, she turned back to face me, her eyes widened in seeming fear, like she'd just recalled she had an audience. "I'm sorry," she added on cue, her pants down by her ankles—figuratively, of course.

Might as well have a sense of humor. If you're going to break rules, the so-called frame of treatment, you'll be met with surprises, and surprises are funny. Moreover, surprises generate illusions, which are alternatively described by Winnicott (1951) as a feature of self-comfort, play, and creative experience. As humans, our capacity for illusion is our mind's reach into the world. It is our gift of fantasy, standing as a third principle of mental functioning, between Freud's (1911) primary process or pleasure principle, and the "objective" reality principle or secondary process. For him, illusions were unhealthy, enabling slavish adherence to rituals, religion. For others, it's a salutary calling: the pull of your hometown football team; the die-hard love of your favorite rock and roll band. For Winnicott, the pejorative term *delusion* applied when individuals impose the subjectivity of their “illusionment” on others, demanding that others see things as they do. Further, when individuals are subject to rigid authority, like when adolescents feel compelled to accept adults’ perceptions of reality, the result is a deadening of thought and fantasy. Likewise, when faced with patients who exhibit fixed ideas that fill the analytic space, squeezing out any sense of another’s subjectivity, a treatment episode can seem dead in the water. We stop caring. Hope is renewed if we can endure disappointments and impotence yet continue wanting and dreaming; otherwise, disillusionment shatters or consumes. But we can hang in there, waiting for something to happen, like a parapraxis or some other surprise return of a repressed element. Return of the repressed: sounds like a bad idea for a book or movie title, a *Star Wars* spin-off destined to bomb at the box office. We don’t know if Freud shared a joke with the Rat Man after telling him he liked him. Nor do I know if laughing with (or at) Naomi was the moment that broke the ice between us and caused her to start feeling better or, even critically, about the future.

Illusion speaks to analyst desire, which, as Wilson (2003) writes, is unconscious, unlike wishes, which are specific and more readily identified. Philips (2024) reminds us that in the Freudian story what we most want is what we must not have, so we inhibit, play hide-and-seek, compromise, maneuver, amuse, give up. Not wanting deadens but keeps us alive. What do we *want*? Consciously, displacing our ghostly taboos, reducing and disguising our aims, we want to establish our control cases, get them approved by our supervisors, graduate our programs, and upon finishing earn the privilege to call ourselves psychoanalysts. Beyond that prestige, our desire is fragile, illusory, procreative, at times fantastic, or enigmatic. And so it is to our patients, surely. Wilson writes that patients are ever on the lookout for our agendas, what we appear to want for them, or ourselves, whether we are neutral in our stances and demeanor or accommodating in some way that arouses curiosity or suspicion. A patient whose fee has been slashed or whose needs for scheduling changes has been met may wonder aloud how we are benefiting from their treatment. Why are we putting up with them four times per week for an indeterminate period? What’s in it for us? At times we may hold our breath, wondering if patients are onto us, having somehow researched our identities and discovered our candidacy, if we haven’t already disclosed that status. Some, perhaps most, candidates in training keep the fact of their analytic training a secret. It’s not like the stage of prelicensed practice wherein disclosure of training status is required. Would patients feel used if they knew the truth? Would they feel privileged to have been chosen as a special case?

Depending on their preconceptions or their attention to cultural or media stereotypes, patients might associate psychoanalysts with revered or feared figures in society: teachers, coaches, authority figures of one kind or another, members of the priesthood, especially if the auras of isolation and abstinence are known. We are Saint Peters, blessing a passage to heaven, absolving of guilt and of wanting something more. We are like the gatekeeper in Kafka's *Before the Law*: stolid figures, telling patients that the entrance to the law is for them and only them, but entrance is ever denied; sessions end with answers remaining hidden. Patients might find their analysts withholding and severe, like a gothic elder or like Whistler's mother, sitting austerely in a chair, listening quietly, detached. Capacities of patience, wisdom, and emotional restraint are often assigned to the analyst in the patient's imagination. We possess a deep reservoir of compassion, a seeming imperturbable air, though our approval or disapproval is ambiguous. For some, we may seem like serene bartenders who don't drink, or don't drink anymore. It's not that we don't know about life. We listen and we take the patient's money and we watch the patient drink and stagger from their stools without judgment; meanwhile, the patient forms the impression that we do this thing, play this wallflower role, instead of doing what they are doing and what we might have done once upon a time until it nearly killed us. Let 'em wonder about that, we exude, keeping the truth about ourselves close to our chests.

The Patient's Imagination and Unconscious

Then there's the analyst's imagination and unconscious, ready to play as the door to the office opens and the patient walks in. The game, of an aesthetic if investigatory kind, begins: from that moment forward all actions are relevant; all thoughts are linked, Freud taught (1915). A patient has come to understand conceptually that his habitual actions act on anxiety; they displace anxiety from some other source, generating anxiety that is lesser than that which is deep in their mind. Incest? They wouldn't be aware of that. A less taboo consideration is that habitual actions, obsessive tendencies, create distance, exhibit fear of closeness. The exhibit is there for the analyst to notice, so we point out that an obsessive tangent seems like a moving away from something. The patient shrugs. Having previously understood the concept, they haven't necessarily learned to notice their defenses as they occur "live." Almost invariably, another opportunity arises that calls for the analyst's attention and something else: a capacity, a stroke of creativity, and possibly genius, to notice a slip or a link, or both, depending on which mechanism gets privileged in the noticing. The patient speaks of a transient encounter and chuckles as they say, "I was taken care of." Here the analyst eschews use of humor so as to isolate its use by the patient. The analyst observes the chuckle and remarks on the interesting turn of phrase, suggesting a desire that is hidden or brushed off.

It's our responsibility to know our desire, which includes our moral principles, or to attempt to know it since it is an unconscious part of us. This can be confusing when our desire for a patient becomes blurred with their desire. A patient who is more than cooperative says something like, "I know you don't want me to . . . ," and mock rolls their eyes, signifying a grudging compliance. Thinking this a Superego defense, an "I should" that reveals slavish desire for authority, we might intervene by pointing out that the desire of the patient is lost in an expression that makes another's wishes a priority. Someone else is taking responsibility for the idea: a problem, for one is moved to rebel if the idea is someone else's. That idea lands, kind of, as the twitchy glances betray continued confusion. The signal of awareness remains scrambled, and another few passes over this defensive front will be necessary to make something that is slippery conscious. Meanwhile, we take in a fair if tacit protest: the glazed look of the patient challenges us to consider that we may indeed want them to stop doing the behavior that they think we want them to stop. Now they're wondering what this treatment is. What's the deal here? Is the analyst in charge? Echoing Freud (1915), we think the patient is meant to idealize us, perhaps fall in love with us, in order for a proper engagement in treatment to occur. But they're also meant to differentiate, not be required to submit. At the outset of treatment, our informed consent statements may have spoken to what is promised and what isn't. Writing of case reports that recruit patient opinion, Stoller (1988) thinks that consent can't possibly cover all that might happen in analysis; some phenomena, including outcomes, are simply unpredictable.

We think we're meant to restrain desire, focus instead on a patient's goals, meet them where they're at, and so on. Our task is to be neutral so as to allow space for thinking and to make less likely a mere compliance with authority. Restraining our desire is akin to therapeutic abstinence—we renounce, or as Freud (1913) recommended, we're supposed to provide evenly hovered attention, not looking to hear anything in particular or to rebuke something preconceived as forbidden or unhealthy. The resistant patient will perceive these agendas from a mile away, our supervisors warn us. Their instruction seems transparent. Help. Be helpful, and in being helpful, be aware of your own needs but prepare to sacrifice them. Sacrifice? What is this, a religion? Freud would not have liked that. He espoused a method of scientific inquiry, emphasizing interpretation, which leads us to observe *why* patients behave as they do or think what they think and to enjoin them in that curiosity. This represents our shared hermeneutic need: to find meaning, and meaning seeking transcends a mere adherence to rules, which in turn can obviate the making of meaning. But what of other needs, our narcissistic needs, like our need as analysts to be recognized, to receive gratitude if a patient's life improves, to get credit, maybe even charge a commission based on a composite metric of patient improvement? Okay, maybe not that. But perhaps lack of recognition is the reason we are sometimes frustrated that psychoanalysis gets co-opted by derivative therapeutic models, that psychoanalysis hasn't bothered to research itself more or promoted the movement as a standard-bearer of mental health care. As candidates, we observe something contradictory in our training: We are immersed in the most time-consuming, most expansive and rigorous course any of us could have imagined. Meanwhile, the model of psychoanalysis seems beset with a monastic, self-defeating ethos: it claims reticence about its own knowledge because an experience of knowing is itself something to repress.

The humility of that ethos, or the fear buried within it, is meant to temper our desire. It stops us from being pedantic, or otherwise insistent upon what patients are meant to improve or understand from our interpretations. That likely means that we won't get the credit for change that we covet, and we're meant to keep that disappointment—that possible disillusionment—to ourselves. A maverick retort, like that of Renik (1994), would suggest that this position is wrongheaded because analysts' interpretations are not meant to represent truisms anyway but rather to stimulate the analytic development of patients; besides, again, our agendas, which include our feelings, will inevitably become known to them, eventually. Ostensibly, we observe this development when we hear our interpretations fed back to us, digested, or half digested perhaps, and therefore returning in an altered form because they have been filtered through an ego that may be differentiating from us as well as the objects on which we are based. At first, we might think this is a mistake. The patient has misunderstood us. They have taken our interpretations and run with them, mutilating them in the process. Was this meant to happen? We wonder confusedly. Again, who is in charge here? Who's getting paid? If patients are performing their own thinking, what is our role? To merely witness and mutely absorb? And if the stage of idealization for the sake of engagement has passed, and understanding us has evolved asymmetrically into a phase of us understanding them, then what else is there for us to do? What else would we want from this weird arrangement?

Long before this mooted stage of analytic arrival, patients seem more needy and unaware; they are dependent yet resistant, hungry yet refusing food. Figuratively, we hold a spoon to their lips, invite an oral opening, and then unperturbably watch as they swat away our thoughts and speak past us, barely aware they are doing that. They want something sweet and sugary, not our sparse diet of vegetables. Tell us what to do, they invariably appeal. Encourage us, tell us what we're good at, what we're doing right. Be positive for a change—*for* a change? Reassure us that everything will be all right if we just stay the course and do as we are told. Nod a lot, or say "hmm" affirmingly when we can't see you from the couch. Let us know that you're listening and that what you hear from us is good stuff, important thinking. The patients: they're children, we learn as candidates. Candidates: we're children, we learn as candidates. We've got a long way to go, so stay the course. Actually, the pull to encourage or compliment is no joke. In early treatment especially, the pressure to make the patient feel better instead of getting better is immense. The pressure's coming from patients, plus the world outside; the mainstream thought of positive thinking, of saying encouraging, warm things to people, gets streamed into the cloister of psychoanalysis and at least threatens hegemony. Our institutes, our supervisors, and our fledgling peers all have our backs on this matter, which is a good thing because the social forces lined up against us are potent, vociferous, and less precariously established these days.

For instance, the 12-step recovery movement, which is about a generation younger than psychoanalysis, is known to provide a great deal of encouragement, validation, and gratification of emotional needs. For an alcoholic in an AA meeting, abstinence has a singular meaning: don't drink. Besides this suggestion, the helpers, which are peers and not professional, knowing but not expert in the scientific sense, offer a group experience that is antidotal to social isolation. The afflicted figure in this milieu has hitherto lived a life of secrecy and dishonesty, placing faith in substances, in acting out versus reflective thought. Thinking is considered dangerous: a setup for calculated machination, resting on a foundation of disordered personality, "character defects." My early introductions to Kohut, Winnicott, and Masterson in proto-analytic seminars seemed to complement the 12-step ethos: the therapeutic task is one of mending deficits, not interpreting internal conflict. The spirit of a spirit would take the pressure off. "Letting go," in surrender to a higher power, such as a deity, is the prescription, alongside regular meeting attendance. In joining this fellowship, a member submits to a group and an enveloping philosophy, and despite not paying money for a service provided, such members expect instruction and some manner of social reward. Report a stretch of abstinence from a habit, even a single day of not using drugs or drinking, and they'll receive warm applause and a token gift as acknowledgment. Confess to a slip or a relapse, and they'll hear promises of day and night support: call us anytime, say fellow members, designated sponsors. The struggling newcomer—so called because of relapse status, not because they are unfamiliar—is the most important figure in the group, says the program ethic. The rest must spread the word, carry a message, and do so with unswerving encouragement and gently instructive fervor. Some members are concurrent participants in psychotherapy or even psychoanalysis. As helpers to others, they may adopt stances that are compatible with analytic thinking, such as taking a neutral, undemanding position with respect to newcomers. However, while mindful of keeping safe distance from toxic involvements or from counterproductive efforts to control uncontrollable addictions, most 12-step helpers do not perceive a need to question their helping motives. Generally, they view their efforts as sanguinary and commonly altruistic, not defensive against an unconscious guilt.

Neutrality may be a beaten and bullied construct for some, a resilient, indispensable analytic commodity for others. Itinerantly discussed, it has toured the world of psychoanalysis and beyond, has a residency at institutes

in San Francisco, New York, Los Angeles, London, Buenos Aries, wherever . . . Lisbon. This stretch of text is where several names and dates are meant to line up as an inventory of prominent thought on the subject at hand. Not doing that. Apparently, Anna Freud (1936) gave a widely regarded definition when neutrality was deemed the cornerstone of analytic technique: the analyst remains equidistant from the psychic agencies of id, ego, and Superego. In other words, keep an equal proximity to pleasure, reality, and the demands of society. Neutrality is a hard-fought position, personally staked out. We take a look, a long look, at what we want for our patients, for ourselves. We've floundered in analysis, in supervision, to answer the question: What do we want? What can we locate within ourselves that we can then abstain from, park somewhere for later use, or just let go? Sometimes, we come up with something, maybe something generic and banal like wanting to help people; sometimes we confess to something more self-serving, indulgent, like the desire to feel important, to impress, or even to entertain. Or it'll be something a bit darker or shameful, like the desire for a peaceful life, earning a modest income with our modest share of social prestige. This desire for a peaceful life, absent of conflict, betrays itself in careless niceties. We contrive a last organizing thought for a patient who won't leave until they've grasped a takeaway piece of wisdom. It'll make 'em feel good, maybe, or at least good about us, the process of treatment, as they walk away.

Neutrality seems to be about knowing, or trying to know what we want, and then not acting on that wanting. It's a cousin to abstinence. It's like saying, "Our time's up," not seizing the last authoritative, sage words of a session, but then adding, "I'll see you tomorrow," because the conversation, the thinking, will continue, just with breaks. Perhaps this idea of neutrality relates to character, as Grossman (2022) writes of it. It's the analyst's makeup, their individualistic, subjective attitude, that determines what they hear and say to a patient, not so much theory, much less science or the influence of the arts. Maybe Freud, Klein, Bion, or whoever else from the past would have agreed with that thought. Maybe Philips, Maroda, Renik, Wilson, or whoever else from our present age would agree with that thought. Is there anything else? Anything more? There's always something more, we think. It's how we started this thing after all: wanting "more." Well, there are the intangibles of identity, of being ourselves, whatever that means. To thine own self be true, said the father to the son—therefore, ideas, or opinions, which may be like ideas only harder and more fixed, someone said and maybe wrote. Being ourselves means style, which suggests something irreducible and personal, or as supervisors sometimes offer, something not to be tampered with. It seems like something that is given free rein in training, or at least room to breathe. It is our effusive energy or our reserved demeanors. Or style is unspecific as a statement; it might represent a broad swathe of stances. Style is in our diction, in our turn of phrase, our tendency to be blunt, earthy, or pally in our manner of address, or, if we prefer, it is our affinity for softness, for impeccable expression, and therefore formality, the preservation of order and tradition.

Humor is a rebel feature of analytic identify, a figure denied entry, it seems. Freud (1905) wrote that jokes are disguised hostility, representing something to be analyzed. That suggests something diagnostic, something that ought to be purged from the process of treatment, and perhaps most analysts would agree with that position. Or not. In analytic circles, as in seminars, conferences, or social gatherings that are peripheral to analytic culture, humor seems genteelly practiced for the most part, understated and careful. Few speak of how they use humor in one other arena of analysis: the analytic space that is the office. Bader (1993), for one, wrote about it, more or less echoing Renik in the view that humor is a feature of emotion and therefore something inevitably shared with a patient at some point. Still, when we sit in our offices, alone or with a patient, and we hear through our office walls the sound of a colleague's and patient's laughter—especially if it's uproarious or persistent—we wonder at least if something inappropriate is happening, if someone's breaking the rules, having too much fun. Psychoanalysis is not meant to be pleasurable and so on. In professional circles, flippancy is deemed a problem: a distasteful, irreverent acting out. Sometimes this attitude seems prudish. Stop being so . . . so abstinent, we want to say. Or some of us want to say, I should say. Satire is revolutionary and therefore dangerous. Humor calls out the elephant in a room—a room we must nonetheless read carefully. In this text, humor is an impish wild dog, poking its nose in the backyard and disturbing the chickens. Ruffling feathers. A euphemism for predation, murder? It's interesting that humor can seem direct or indirect: an avoidance of a problem, soothing nerves; alternatively, it cuts like a knife, efficiently naming truth.

Truth seeking is a powerful, perhaps insidious, justifier. Humor can be rationalized if it cuts through . . . ya know. I repress. I repress an aspect of style, a vulgarity, but not the message. It is merely tidied, cleaned up a bit. Is that a lie? Some might think so. But again, maybe truth, and therefore humor, need only signal its presence, not take over and assume authority. Back to Shakespeare: in *King Lear*, humor is in the fool who represents truth waiting in the wings but occasionally making itself heard. Sometimes we think absurdity, or the attention drawn to absurdity, is the only way of breaking through denial, especially when it's the denial of leaders. We can do this with peers also if we don't mind risking ostracism. Holden does it with his Pencey roommate Ackley, who won't stop jabbering when Holden's trying to read a book. Ackley punctuates his spiel by asking about the book, whether Holden likes it, to which Holden replies: "This sentence I'm reading is terrific." Ackley didn't get it, Holden's sarcasm. Humor doesn't always break through obtuseness, denial. Breaking through denial: our categorical imperative, maybe—only we'll choose our method based on who we think we are. Whether who we are achieves truth is ambiguous, complicated, yet we maintain a Kantian ethic. Or it's a Kantian aesthetic, to seek truth in a style of our choosing. Doing no harm, playing it safe, is another categorical imperative, so we have choices, not easy choices, about who we are, what role to play and how to play it in any given context. Here's one:

I sit with a handful of Rat Man–ish men in a group therapy context. Groups are a different animal in analysis. Rats in packs—that's another subject. In this vignette, group means collusion, the dodging of conflict, and the group leader—in this case myself—is a provocateur. A man speaks ambiguously of health concerns, long-standing problems with dizziness, unsteady gait, feelings of physical weakness. He's been consulting with his doctor on these problems for months, possibly longer, but has no answers; no specific diagnosis or prescription has been forthcoming. Amid a problem-solving-like exchange between this man and the group, he eventually reveals a relevant factor: he's been smoking marijuana daily—an increase in use since his casual, less frequent use of the substance was previously known to everyone. Is this a cause of his difficulty, the group wonders? A factor in exacerbating symptoms perhaps? Nobody knows, but one or two chime in with a commonsense suggestion: tell your doctor. Then the first man springs a twist: "Don't wanna," he says, familiarly terse. It's his style. It's also a reflection of a familiar angst: his anxiety, even paranoia, about medical authority. He has deficits, I think. "I don't want that going on my record," he reluctantly adds. Having been here before, fellow group members attempt to circumvent the defense, speaking to their perceptions of reality. They don't think revelation of marijuana use will compromise his medical benefit. No one in the group, which is composed of similarly distrustful figures, has ever heard of such a thing. The man is unmoved. I try a different tack that stills the group into silence, one of those awkward silences by my estimation: "So your fear of authority is more important to you than a potential threat to your health, leading you to hold back from your doctor what may be crucial information." "I guess so," the man replies with a placid smile but a stubborn air. I continue: "You may be more concerned about your marijuana use than you're aware of. Plus, you supplied this information to us. You didn't have to. No one asked about it beforehand." Someone said I was trying to make him feel guilty—that old chestnut. Actually, my purpose was even more basic: to show to him (and the group) that we were important to him. Anyway, the group tries one other tack, that of suggesting separate, as in online, research into the question of marijuana use and its possible link to the man's symptoms. They think this a worthy compromise, an action of therapeutic reasoning. It also

implies an original idea, as if the task of researching the question online had never occurred to the man before, or further, that learning disturbing information would necessarily alter his position. In truth, my truth, I became frustrated, impatient with the process—the seeming failure, in my view—of social response to problems. As the group session wound down to a close, platitudes filled the air: let's keep an open mind, keep researching the issue. The man readily agreed, as this was committing him to nothing. Someone raised their hand like they were in a class, volunteering to do research on the man's behalf, as if knowing the man's passivity but not concerned with that as a problem in itself. The group concluded on a virtue-signaling note: let's check our facts, keep seeking information. "That's fine, gentlemen. Anyway, we're at time for tonight," I said, unsatisfied. Someone broke into this abrupt end—not an unusual event either—with a "quick" question for me on the topic that afforded a response I didn't abstain from: "Well, I'll look into that too. I'll also check whether smoking helps when you're running and out of breath."

Chapter 4
Identity

Style may be therapeutic but not analytic. Style is meant to evolve toward identity. Merge. At times, it can feel draining, as if something is being lost. If hard fought, there will be bleeding. Time to write more about me. As I wrote earlier, when I started work as a psychotherapist 20-plus years ago, I thought I was a versatile practitioner. Upon reflection, I am less and less sure what that means, the bit about confrontational stances notwithstanding. Work settings shaped me, governed what I did and thought. Remember, they're never in the room with you, one supervisor said to me back when I was starting out. She was referring to peers, other supervisors, directors, even administrators. Her purpose was to stir thoughts in me as to what kind of therapist I wanted to be. What kind of identity was I cultivating, regardless of social or institutional influence? I will have nodded agreeably, lacking an answer but willing to give the matter headspace. Was I doing something wrong? I was locked in binaries, conscious of my fledgling status, my learner's ethos. The context was alcohol and drug treatment, which was all about taking in the messages of others, which was well privileged over speaking out, much less speaking back. Versatility? As much as anything, that will have meant doing whatever it takes, or claiming to do whatever's necessary, to demonstrate being down for the group, the cause. To please authority. As for confrontational stances, that was about authority also, about telling patients who seemed to lack authority—social, legal, or moral—that they'd traded their futures for short-term pleasures. Their present days were about loss, much like their pasts were.

Warnings. As counselors in this environment, my peers and I were professional warners first and deep-psyche divers a distant second. We were team players, frontline foot soldiers, seed planters. The seeds were thoughts, as in cognitions, though the theoretical underpinnings were vaguely psychodynamic. Via observation, I thought patients exhibited critical thinking errors, had "distorted cognitions," as some would have put it. The premises of their assertions were off base, were presumptuous and biased. Therefore, the syllogisms of their thinking—*You care for me; therefore, you will . . .* —were problematic. However, it seemed from the outset of my career that such distortions were not rooted in intellectual limitations but rather personal experience. Though I didn't formulate problems in psychoanalytic terms, I in effect gleaned that the emotional conflicts and pathological symptoms of patients were Oedipal in nature (problems relating to inhibition and reactions against inhibition) or else were borne of constitution or preverbal development (splitting defenses, projective identification).

Transferentially, in a residential setting, counselors are aunts and uncles, temp foster parents. As for the patients, they were imps and wounded birds, or in some cases villains. Their purpose, we were told, was to "test" us, which meant usurping our authority, or at least mocking or circumventing it. That was their job, we were told by those with experience. It was not a collaboration, this bond, this contract, between patient and clinician. It was an opposition, a battle. So, for a while anyway, I became a twitchy scold, nervously playing quasi-parent to a handful—a caseload, it was dubbed—of troubled people. To distance from the personal, the dangers of getting too close to the subject, our patients were as often as not called cases. The leaders of this agro-ambience were steely eyed, hard-nosed (or hard-limbed) drug treatment veterans who reminded me of childhood pop heroes. What comes to mind are the odd fireman or rescue person I once knew, or a policeman neighbor, but the daily dramas of such people were unknown to me, sheltered as I was. Easier to reference and draw meaning from are the fictional stand-ins. A memorable and illustrative one was a disaster flick titled *The Towering Inferno* featuring a pair of blue-eyed, blondish doppelgangers: Paul Newman and Steve McQueen.

They seemed like two versions of the same person. Newman played the first hero: a rugged ladies' man, an alpha male equally loved by the guys, elegant and eloquent, yet with a hint of neurosis. In the film's plot, he is at first aloof, in denial about the disaster that looms over a skyscraper he has designed that will later burn through the night, hence the title. As the story unfolds, he becomes more engaged, takes more responsibility; he learns as he goes, takes the hero's journey, and delivers half the moral at the end. The other half of the lesson is delivered by McQueen's fire chief, more of a working-class hero: straight talkin', blunt, unfriendly, uncharming, sweatier and dirtied by his job but solid as a rock, not in denial about anything. He sees all dangers, knows what to do, and as he does his job he will sneer at or lament what he already knows rather than learn. As a 16-year-old, I'd have aspired to Newman's persona, to be more winning with women especially in my nonviolent everyday life. This was the sanguine youth in me, believing in the "magic" of cinema, before Holden Caulfield scolded me through literature, saying that movies don't mean shit. As an eight-year-old, I wanted to be the other guy in the cheesy disaster flick: to know everything, not feeling weak or vulnerable. As an aspiring therapist working in hospital-based drug treatment, I wanted to be like the firemen-types among the staff. Consciously, and therefore publicly, I'd have paid lip service to learning, to not knowing much and therefore needing help in order to help others. Beneath that, I longed to be a know-it-all.

Being prepared versus careless: seeing problems, anticipating dangers, not being arrogant or narrow-minded and therefore careless. These were some of the morals within the scripts of mine and others' counsel. Like the road-tested fire chief, we'd say go for it, keep building higher and higher, but remember: safety first. Styles varied, of course, and not everyone among staff was heavy-handed or myopic with dire warnings for our miscreant patient population. As a mini-cultural milieu, we believed in good old-fashioned, tried-and-true therapeutic tools: urging patients to make apologies when they behaved badly, encouraging others to forgive them in return. Assert yourself when your needs and desires are appropriate, but calm your reckless self when greedy. Stay in the present day with day-to-day tasks, but think about the future, the prospect of a stable if modestly risk-taking life. That sort of thing. Was there anything from the profession-founding crypt of psychoanalysis in the mix of hospital-based drug treatment? Yes, quite a lot actually, albeit in cloaked form. A sort of proto-analysis existed in the form of exploration of past behavior and past relationships. Charismatic counselors, people who liked to inject a little drama therapy into their technique, favored "empty chair" exercises, opportunities for patients to exorcise implicitly buried resentments toward absent objects, especially those wayward figures who had modeled the problem behaviors in the first place.

Building patients up was generally deemed therapeutic, as in helpful—being strength-based in approach, observing what someone was good at, not just their flaws or defenses. Regularly, we implied seeing the good, the strong, the ordinarily if not extraordinarily ambitious qualities in patients, but we also observed inhibition. Long before I'd read Freud's (1926) thoughts about symptoms, inhibitions, and anxiety, I'd thought that patients with destructive habits, like addictions, experience conflict between desire and inhibition. Their pleasure-achieving activities serve drive but also ego defense, serving as a compromise. The problem drinker finds pleasure or at least relief in their binges, but they also subdue feelings like anger, with conflict avoidance, escapism, leading to abrogated responsibility and thwarted goal seeking. A patient is passive in their daily life, often failing to say no to what they don't want, or really going for what they actually want instead—even with goals that are socially acceptable, like education or career seeking or wholesome, mutually loving relationships. Paradoxically, they chose the rebellion of acting out, instances of pleasure seeking, poor impulse control, instead of being truly active in their lives, building a core purpose. Having *agency*, we might call this. That "just say no" thing that our culture now mocks as a drug use prevention strategy: many who struggle being active versus passive do indeed fail to "just say no," but not just to drugs. They struggle across contexts. Reading contemporary analytic thinkers like Masterson (1976, 1981) and later Brenner (1981), Director (2005), and Dodes (2003) helped me shape the view that a dialectic between omnipotence and helplessness forges internal conflict. I was formulating about my patients, and through the patients I was treating I was gradually developing, albeit unwittingly, an analytic identity.

A point here is that much of this analytic development happens before the onset of "full" analytic training. For some readers, that may seem like a misguided, audacious point of view, though for many others it may seem like nothing less than commonplace perspective. Participating in personal analysis, traversing years of seminar and case supervision, one feels over time a sense of discovery, not creation per se: ideas click like those of an *apres coup*; these things we learn as candidates, we felt them all along, before we even began analytic training. Analytic lessons, the theoretical ideas we learn to articulate, have been imbued in everyday life for as long as we could remember. They were in our play as kids, in our trials at school, within our family constellations. They were encoded in social events, historical happenings; they were even manifest in the bricks and mortars we inhabited, and they were certainly present when we started toiling in what we broadly term mental health care. Prior to training, psychoanalysis sort of seeps into a budding clinician. One learns latter-day jargon, the concepts that are derivative of repetition compulsion or projective identification, for example, before reading of the original doctrine. And because psychoanalysis does not appear fiercely proprietorial, it is quiet when other models steal its ideas and thunder.

So I toiled in mental health care, in its fraught tide pools, its places of apprenticeship, and moved through the ranks of substance use treatment—actually it was more of a sideways, 60-degree incline than a ladder—but eventually I left my long-standing place of employment, or it left me, as a president once quipped of his former party. I no longer fit into the structure of workplaces, having gained enough experience and knowledge to stop saying or evincing that I didn't know things. Having dodged the layers of administration where institutional fires are lit, I was left scrambling at the exit, seeking career survival at first and then that elusive something more. I found fresh air in the seemingly more genteel world of private practice, where water-cooler conversations are fewer and coffee talk has to be arranged between packed schedules. Here a team ethic, a recruitment into a systemic way of being—your putative identity in a collaborative world—may be extolled, but it is less thickly hegemonic. It begins in its material frame and, as ever, in numbers. Your first sublet is a paltry space, just about bigger than a walk-in closet, barely big enough for an analyst's couch. Your time in the office is limited; you have no parking space yet, and your name on the directory is in small letters.

As you build up your practice, you eventually land in your full-time nest, and then you truly set out your stall. You smile and nod in passing at your office floor mates, as they are no longer suite mates, much less coworkers, people who may be a step or two higher on the professional A-frame. Cursorily, you ask after their practice, and they reciprocate, but verbose jargon prevails in these oft-transient exchanges. They're not here to tell you what to do or how to be, and as you breathe easier with this recognition, you realize the reverse is also true. Theoretically, you are areligious: you've developed some of your own ideas, techniques, or style, drawn from a palette of sources, not from the word of whomever. If you do not adhere to that which is deemed cutting-edge, meaning that which is sourced from the previous five years, you may be marginal, but it will be a muted shunning; referrals may be sparse. You have ethical standards—indeed, many that are deeply felt—but you are not moralistic in the sense that you or your patients are going to some kind of hell for not complying with societal norms. If you think analytically, or proto-analytically, you think in psychological dimensions not moral ones: it's more about what people think and why versus what they should say or do.

You're in isolation. I, you, we, the impersonal one, and they, are in isolation—together, if you've experienced this or you're planning on it. In analytic training, most candidates are in private practice, though some appear tethered to systems, especially hospitals. We are midcareer or in some cases early career, while a sparse few are at the tail end of their working days. Most have aspired, at least, to professional individuation. Therefore, the private practice model, distanced to varying degrees from oversight, seems the norm that shapes our thinking. We're positioned toward the isolated pole in a dialectic between individualism and the values of the group. We've known the platitudes: individualize treatment, treatment plans, but don't treat patients as if they live in vacuums. Recognize society, and beyond that a social unconscious. The isolation of private practice threatens to separate us, keep us split from society, bosomed in niches even, with patient populations that reflect our interests, which may become narrowed. In these pockets, we can become pockets, can write books (like I have) about specialized problems, like sex addiction, and target our audience. We market. And what we market is a demi-expertise, as well as promises. Early in treatment, we're not much different from electricians, plumbers, lawyers, or financial advisers, the people who talk about numbers mostly. Analysts—we don't have numbers for the consumer, as in days or number of sessions required for resolution of a problem. We steer clear of promises, suggest commitment and patience. We offer abstractions. Insurance may have numbers bound by limits (number of sessions authorized) that imply when a problem should be solved. Or insurance is like a cold parent saying enough is enough when a child turns 18. You can go on if you like—go "deeper"—but you're on your own now.

Training brings us back to groups: to the classroom; to one-on-one arrangements (supervision) that conjure prototypes of coaching, mentoring; to an institute that houses a community of thought and gathers recruits. It, this institute, makes few promises, ensures nothing to speak of. You can meet requirements—attend classes, treat patients, and navigate those rigorous multi-session-per-week control cases, write a good paper after seminar's complete—and graduate, but then you're on your own still. Of course, the same could be said of our patients. We don't offer them much—at least, not much of a concrete or material nature. Those patients who are electricians and plumbers: they in particular notice this. But they're in analysis because they, too, feel isolated. They've been unloading on their customers, they notice. They've been working away, in cramped spaces, feeling it in their knees and in their lower backs, but talking the whole time and getting more personal, getting deeper, with every twist of a wrench. And it feels good, they say, to get a few things off their chest, to exercise a little thought. That is, until they look up at their trapped listeners, some homeowner that stares back at them with an expression that says, *Hey man, I just need my toilet fixed.* Time to pay someone to listen, to do it right. And if we develop one analytic identity above all others, it'll be that of a good listener, a next-level thinker. We won't teach so much, at the end of our working days. The institutes: ultimately, they won't teach so much.

We don't know how far we'll go, how deep, in our personal analyses. We don't know how far our patients will go. We don't know. Some, like those people whose daily lives are mired in numbers, will surprise us, expose our prejudices. They'll want more than to get thoughts off their chest. Like us, they'll want more. Some will ask directly, while others, for complicated reasons—reasons bound up in their lives with objects—will struggle to ask, to communicate, what they want. They inhibit themselves but are unaware of doing so, so their strategies are indirect, inferable at best when illustrated by habit. Take the supposedly dull or boring patient. Their sharing is glib, generic; it lacks substance, glossing over details. Ostensibly, they are sparing their analysts from a dull experience. That is, they're aware of not wanting to "bore" the analyst with minutia, things they presumably won't know or care about. Actually, another possibility is that an analyst might know what's being spoken of and therefore present another problem.

Jerry speaks of team meetings at work with coworkers about projects that were incomplete and behind schedule (no, he's not a plumber or an electrician). He keeps starting to explain a detail of his work only to pull back his thought: "Anyway, that part doesn't matter." At some point, I remark on this habit, speculating that he's wary of telling me the full details of his project, not because they don't matter or because he's sparing me the burden of tracking his dull, convoluted world, but rather because he is wary of my knowing his experience, perhaps knowing it so much that I might disagree with him, contest his narratives.

Possibilities. There are different possibilities for why a patient is speaking in session in a vague, obfuscating, inhibited fashion. The point here is to stay open-minded to possibilities, to the possibilities of our patient's experience as well as our own. I'm told, and I'm coming around to believing this, that my responses, my countertransference responses, are useful barometers of patient resistance; they're at least as much a barometer of patient resistance as they are, say, a reflection of my limitations. A man, an analyst, has to know his limitations, but perhaps we shouldn't assume that our limitations are the dominant cause of phenomena. I can daydream listening to patients like Jerry. I can lose track, then get back on track like a locomotive that can jump when a thought of mine, a thought of the patient, jolts me back to attention. Is that my habit, my lifetime affliction? Yes, I write gingerly, thinking there is much at stake here. But when that habit occurs is not only historical; it is contextual—here today as well as in the past, getting reenacted. I could blame Jerry, offer that others being boring is the cause of attention lapses—the proper reason why analytic and therapy sessions are meant to be only 50 minutes long. Maybe those are details—blame, supposedly natural limits—that don't matter. Perhaps what matters is getting curious, staying curious, about why phenomena like boredom and inattention occur, why inhibition, which yields boredom, has happened, historically and contextually.

Another feature of analytic identity—actually, maybe a prerequisite for candidacy—is the belief that present-day symptoms, neurosis, dissociation, addictions, etcetera, are derivative of early object experience. We reenact in our daily lives, in our relationships. We reenact in analysis. Patients are unaware of this reenactment, or they're thinly aware of it. They may want from us something they didn't get from their objects, like guidance or the tolerance of labile mood states. Listening, and then something more. Some will ask after these goods, tell us to fill in the gaps. Please, they won't say explicitly. They may be wary of rebuke or the more passive rejection of reticence, our seeming withdrawals.

Other models of care, the rivals of psychoanalysis, will claim to fill the gaps that it leaves. Teachers, coaches, mentors, sponsors, and others of nonanalytic ilk will encourage, discourage, guide, criticize, praise, dispense wisdom . . . lead. Famously, psychoanalysts might not do any of these things. Or they may do all of these things from time to time, sparingly, secretly. Why? Because we're not replacing objects. We're only illustrating their importance, absorbing the projections, then explaining their place in the patient's mental economy. Regarding the ubiquity of objects, one case conference instructor offered a question that was meant to steer candidates' thinking throughout the course: where are the patient's objects? Can we hear them in those convoluted, vague shares, within those demands for our flexibility, forbearance, nonjudgment, or instruction?

Sharon thought her parents were always bringing her down. She had ideas, intellectual in nature, that she thought would match their sensibilities, be met with their approval. Instead, they were ever skeptical and discouraging. Their rationales fell under the heading of protection. They worried for Sharon, thought her provocations would get her in trouble at school; they would alienate friends, romantic prospects. Sharon was bemused. She thought or felt that her parents were not so much protective as envious and therefore malevolent. Did they hate her? Did they secretly hate her? Thinly aware of what she projected onto me, needed from me, she was sensitive to my words, their connotations, the sheer sound of them. Otherwise, she'd search for my thought in my expressions, matching them to her associative memory or finding contrast.

This is corollary to a taboo consideration, that parents don't always have their children's best interests at heart, that they feel envy toward children, aggressive impulses that are disguised by the proclaiming of wholesome, caretaking intention. Beyond the confines of psychoanalysis, this may be one of the most provocative theories posed or perhaps just loosely mooted to the general public, despite the ready acknowledgment from many if not most parents that children do indeed provoke exasperation, even rage. But such feelings are like the rivalrous impulses of Jerry in his day-to-day life: they are felt but then smoothed over, diluted. Meanings secondary to frustration, deeper feelings like envy, are repressed. In analysis, they may be projected onto the clinician, who must be wary of their own emergent frustration, either at the parent analysand or at the spoken-of child. Uncomfortable feelings in the patient are assigned to the analyst or are projected onto the analyst, as in the cases of Jerry and Sharon. That boredom in the patient is a contagion. It carries the deadness that feels like suppressed rage. Hear, feel it, take it in. After a few minutes of this, you'll feel it in your eyelids, which want to close. They're shaking, like knees buckling under an unwieldy pressure. Something uncomfortable, even ugly, is being expressed and also transmitted, leading to another impulse: to shut down.

Theories that conceptualize the unconscious desires of a patient, plus that which defends against them, form a part of analytic identity. They serve a way of thinking about how the patient lives and also how they'll show up in the analytic space. Prior to training, not to mention COVID, which nearly coincided in onset, I'd have thought the phrase "analytic space" pretentious. Why not just say office? Now it denotes everything from the therapeutic frame, such as live or telehealth, to something called a field or an analytic "third" to reference some in-between, less definable phenomena that the analytic process generates. This space is bound by a relationship that begins with a consultation, moves an inch with an agreement to follow up, and then to a regular commitment if it's to proceed properly. A patient is impressed by something: they feel safe or they anticipate the pleasure of feeling challenged. Beyond that are certain nodal points: a point of idealization that might arrest progress if it can't shift; a point of crisis—a bad-object experience—that might disillusion, cause rupture if it isn't noticed, spoken of, understood in a way that enables some manner of continuation. Actually, this is true of all experiences along the false continuum of good to bad. The idea of this noticing, this speaking to what's happening, and sometimes not, seems crucial to an analytic process. In plain terms, a psychoanalytic arrangement must be real in so far as it must cover a wide range of experience. On the other hand, if it's to be special, and here we must acknowledge that psychoanalysis is indeed offering what it thinks is *special*, then it must become a unique form of relationship, one that speaks to psychological phenomena that most relationships avoid.

Of course, psychoanalysis isn't the only institution that posits relationship-building so highly among its core principles. A casual scroll through the marketing strategies of any profession that seeks consumers would reveal similar proclamations. But it's equally obvious that no other kind of service provider, even within the field of mental health, offers, much less expects, a commitment of several meetings per week, on more days than not, over an indeterminate spell, with so little reciprocity or gratification of material or physical needs. Psychoanalysis calls for and offers what no other profession provides so brazenly, what no patient of mental health care, even those who begin the process educated on psychoanalytic norms, can fully anticipate, except theoretically. You don't know it, can't know it, until you experience it firsthand, and even then it may bewilder you, make you feel like you've stepped into a hole with no base. Informed consent documents won't outline this arrangement. They can't say when an analytic pairing, whether that's an "alliance" as some describe it or a tacit declaration of war as it may seem at times, has begun. It's like another taboo—to say when a relationship, the "it," has started or when it's floundering. It's like what you're not supposed to say on a first date, an erotically motivated injunction: "I think I can work with you," said a new patient recently, looking pleased. She got up and left immediately, having said this right at minute 50. I think she thought she shouldn't say it, not even know yet what might happen.

Somebody said it. Somebody wrote it. Somebody taught it to me recently, this idea that psychoanalysis is an arrangement in which two people agree to meet and not sleep together. They agree to much more, of course. Patients are looking for their identities, some knowledge of themselves as they seek to fit in or not with relationships, in systems, a cultural milieu that surrounds them. Patients and analysts agree to have meetings that are asymmetrical in as much as they reveal much more about the recipient of care than about the provider—on the surface at least. But under and around the surfaces of polite demeanor, of cooperative language or minimalist self-disclosure, there are two factors that separate an analytic stance and an analytic identity from that of any other kind of professional helper: first, a belief that unconscious processes are operating constantly and are revealed in the patient's actions, spoken words, and thoughts that aren't shared; and second, that these unconscious processes will manifest in the transference moments in analysis and that each moment that is recognized as such is an opportunity for an analyst to speak to what is happening in the relationship between analyst and analysand, as proximate to these moments as possible, in the office, in the analytic space. In this way, analysts refute the reputations they have with the nonanalytic world, namely, that they are impersonal, a "blank slate" in presentation, and unavailable for relationship. Quite the contrary: an analyst is more relational—that is, more likely to speak to relational phenomena—than anyone most people are likely to meet in a lifetime.

It's remarkable how frequent the opportunities come around, especially given how constant the underlying transference really is. Before analysis, as an analyst or a subject of it, it is more difficult to notice what is at and around or beneath a surface. Analysis provides a space and exercises an old muscle that has been long dormant. Awakened, it sees around corners, sees in between words; making associations, it links phrases to memory, makes play of what otherwise might seem coincidental. In analysis, there are no "mistakes," as in no slips, that aren't meaningful. Recalling Freud (1915), we understand there is no "no" in the unconscious, no censor. There are no words that are simply misspoken; no gestures that should be ignored, only those that have crossed a repression barrier that we may choose to ignore. Analysts likely develop selective attention patterns. In the interests of economy, they'll leave some phenomena unremarked on, perhaps with the rationale that if all or most phenomena are repetitive, then there will be other moments, other days, in which to deliver interpretations, because to deliver all at once or relentlessly over a stretch of time is too much. It floods the market of a mind, outstripping demand. Evidence for interpretations being excessive, a rationale for letting some phenomena pass without comment concerns patient resistance. Patient resistance is a given, candidates are instructed in training, and being repetitive is annoying. It belittles, makes people feel too young, like children. Strange that we're attracted to repetition given its potential for getting old, so to speak.

This picking our moments thing, exercising something about time, as in timing, is important for reasons that seem elusive. We may think it has something to do with readiness, or more specifically, the readiness of unconscious matter sitting at the gate of awareness. Is it *time* to break through? Flexibly, we might return to the matter of flexibility, considering its application to a range of clinician-patient phenomena. A patient has requests, sometimes demands, that we may or may not wish to meet: they have a fee in mind, a notion of how often they'd like to meet. We're not accommodating enough, perhaps. We might not lower our fee or be flexible with a cancellation policy a patient finds unreasonable. We may not be available often enough, or we may recommend a higher frequency than a patient can tolerate, or than they think they can tolerate. They may want to have relatively impromptu, shortened sessions during a week to supplement fuller sessions—something that will consolidate understanding of a previous hour. They may want to phone an analyst on off days, text the analyst between sessions, offering updates on matters "worked on" in treatment. They may want marathon sessions of several hours, thinking analysis is akin to a hallucinogenic drug trip—something that will hasten the process, create therapeutic highs, well-managed lows. Or they may want back-to-back hours because they believe it takes them longer to delve deep into their feelings and they are irritated by the analytic suggestion that a patient consider why this is the case rather than simply having more time, as the request makes clear. More is better, they might imply. Is less more? Some might think so. Faster, as in reaching goals faster, is better, more people think. Above all, consumers may think that a person getting paid should accommodate the consumer's reasonably formulated and stated needs.

Who do we blame for this? Marshall Field? Customer service is a notion that dominates retail and has at least infiltrated hospital systems and mental health care. There's a term other than *customer service* that has been used in recent times on the websites of health-care providers, especially the big-system ones that promote what they call "partnership plans," downgrading expertise and authority. Conveniently, I've forgotten the term, signifying my resistance to an identity I don't want to inhabit. See, I chose to be a therapist. Now I'm choosing to be an analyst, whether I make it as one or not. I haven't chosen to be a cognitive behavioral therapist, or a ketamine supplier, or a motivational life coach, or some kind of certified something-type therapist that has been given a new name during the time it's taken me to write this book. If I wanted to market myself currently, I might call myself a Sigmund Freud–influenced, Melanie Klein–influenced, Wilfried Bion–influenced, Lance Dodes–influenced, J. D. Salinger–influenced, neo-someone-else psychoanalytic thinker. There may or may not be a niche for such a description, but flippancy aside for at least one passage, there's a wider issue here that bears consideration. As candidates in analytic training, we concurrently operate in a mental health field populated by fragmented identities, analytic and not, and that diaspora of professionals, once homogenized by psychological theory and social assumptions, may still be regarded as homogenized by theory and assumptions by the average consumer of services.

To listen to some who enter treatment, it does not matter one bit whether a therapist is a therapist or an analyst, much less a Kleinian, a Freudian, or a Lacanian, or any other figure who is famous enough to have the suffix *-ian* attached to their name. The average consumer of mental health care is dimly aware that "analysis" entails an in-depth approach linked to ephemera that has been stereotyped by decades of media caricature: an austere, distraction-voided setting, fitted with a couch on which the patient lies, talking to a figure who sits behind them, scribbling notes while sat comfortably, one leg perched atop another, striking an inscrutable air. Advice and advocacy may be sparse, and the interpretations may be oblique. This sets an analyst apart from a therapist, who may employ the same theories about psychopathology, including beliefs about a plethora of neuroses that have been sown in family-of-origin upbringings, but the manner and tone of their interventions is more strident; they are less patient, less observant of a gradual unfolding of change that is interrupted by unconscious dynamics between the patient and the treating professional. There is more gratification in this therapist's approach; less abstaining from self-disclosure, outside-of-session contact; less withholding of encouragement, approval; straightforward as opposed to implied criticism. There is homework borne of an academic paradigm that the patient may readily assign to the process, "tools" with which to improve communication and other generically identified concepts, like self-esteem. In short, there is much more of what average people think helping professionals can and ought to provide to a needful patient.

Good listening. The consumer can and should expect good listening, and on this matter analysts can gratify: listening on another level, listening to that which gets skipped over because it is briefly uttered and moved on from, listening to what is not being said, to what is conspicuously absent, and to that which the analyst might imagine is true based on the inhibited language of the patient. Listening to dreams. Remember dreams? How about daydreams, or better yet reverie, about that which lives in metaphors—uncanny things thought and said aloud. "Funny you say that," says the patient about the interpretation that stirs a link to something thought before by them. The patient who is patient though not necessarily educated about analytic theory may be aware, or at least considerate, that a sort of Heisenberg principle may apply to the analytic process: they are like a particle whose speed and position is hard to fix, signifying uncertainty. Movement, or progress, may stutter or halt, or else escalate in spurts, taking them by surprise, causing exhilaration, then panic, then disappointment as a lull hits and a plateau emerges and smooths out the ride. At the end of the day, the session, or the indeterminate stretch that the unconscious envelops, the patient wants something to change, and if what they want is expansive or ineffable, like an audience with God, they won't care what denomination you are.

These "average people," these mythical everypersons who present for treatment, are composite approximations, perhaps as much unicorn as any control case patient that a candidate covets and strains to hold on to throughout training. Upon navigating a consultation, a would-be analyst and patient agree to work together. Each proceeds wanting their share of freedom, to be what they want to be, who they want to be. The conditions of the world are making these goals hard, we might agree, if comparing life notes. And we're not. But if I'm a priest, don't ask me to play the Buddhist monk. Do your homework, listen; choose me after meeting me, after hearing what I say, how I present myself, what I think treatment is. If I call it psychoanalysis, that's a clue as to what it's not. I won't coach meditation, the meaning of your breath. See if it fits, this other way of thinking that rarely instructs, doesn't sound like anything else. If it sounds weird, a little woo-woo, that's good. That means the patient is attentive, is noticing what's unfamiliar. If they're lost, feeling disembodied, that may not be good. If circumspect, optimally confused but still stringing words together, reaching for a thought that feels as near and distant as a rainbow, that's better. That's me thinking and sometimes speaking to what I want to stir in a patient who has agreed to sit with me for an hour or two before deciding to go further, to find something more. The patient wants freedom also, naturally. That need is in their eyes as they scan the surroundings, taking in what's there and what's not. No less than a surly, midcareer mental health professional, they don't want to be recruited into a system, much less something like an analytic identity. This may be what it means to lie on a couch in a sparsely furnished room and call yourself a patient.

This sense of recruitment recalls what Meltzer (1992) has written on the subject of claustrophobia. Reformulating Klein's (1946) idea of projective identification, Meltzer writes that the inside of the object—in particular the maternal object—is compartmentalized and that the inside of the object can become an entrapping psychic reality, akin to that of a rubbish tip, as the Brit Melzer would have put it, or a concentration camp. A child struggles with separation from a maternal figure, aims to get inside her, take possession of her, follow her as an external object walking away. With projective identification, this phenomenon is also internal, so the child also identifies with the mother, becoming detached, leading to pathological consequences that yield repetitive states of mind activated by separation stressors. Premature independence is a common result, Meltzer writes, leading to poor engagement in intimate relationships in particular. The problem is ripe for the intimacy of an analytic treatment, so patients fall into traps that they have long since internalized when they enter psychoanalysis, taking their analysts down with them, looking to inhabit them, as well as enjoin them in reenactments. What kind of compartment will the analytic space become—what kind of maternal object? The patient struggles to think with the analyst, escape hierarchical structures that families and institutions have cultivated. It is difficult to relax on the couch, not knowing if the unseen figure is there, what the analyst will do to the patient, as Holden feared. It is difficult to start talking about oneself, to play a little, break free of the scaffolding with which they have covered themselves.

A little humor breaks the ice, injecting play or menace, depending on what's internal. Breaks the ice. That's a problem, isn't it? Doesn't it give you a sinking feeling to break through a hard barrier, with either soft tissue or deep water underneath? We've addressed humor here before, covered some bases of what analysts think: humor is hostile, a seductive penetration; it represents defense, a turning away from sincerity to play; or it's protest, necessarily concealed for the sake of safety—the prerogative of the dissenter and underdog, for humor calls out the absurd, deflates pomposity. Except when it's being explained, which makes humor not funny anymore. It's funny, but Freud's 1905 paper "Jokes and Their Relation to the Unconscious" contains two meta-jokes, one of which is that it takes 200 pages to discuss a "technique of a joke." The other is that it was published the same year as *Three Essays*. I can't explain either joke. I get, as in recognize, that my own humor relies heavily on condensed meanings, plays on words, but much of Freud's meaning is elusive to me. He tells joke after joke in "Jokes," most of which I don't get. My thoughts drift as I read, though with luck I'll latch on to a spearing passage that has been quotable for scholars over the last century plus. I wait for the bit where Freud will declare that a joke, unlike a dream, relies for its own significance on being shared, but also that it signifies belonging and understanding. See, it's humor that's helped me feel at home or a part of something, so it's terrible to not "get" a joke.

If it breaks the ice then it's meant to bond people together, make them relax, break the ice that denotes coolness between people. That idea presumes that humor will make people comfortable, which in turn suggests what psychoanalysis is not. So is it nonanalytic to employ humor, sparingly or not? It depends, supervisors or psychoanalytic elders might say. It depends on how one is using it. That's a typical thing for an analyst to say about any open question, and that's me expressing frustration with elliptical thought that leaves space for someone else's answer. That leaving of space is a good thing generally, unless you're actually looking for an answer. So what's the answer on humor? There's no prescribed answer, but there may be an in-between answer, a compromise, for I'd suggest that humor is itself a compromise, if compromise is neither one thing nor another: humor is hostile, a signifier of belonging, of intelligence, or a mere entertainment, perhaps. It may be a welcome mat, signifying a comforting normalcy, to which some might ask, "And why is that so important?" It is a display of frivolity, of play, and yet earnest in its purpose.

Clearly, for some, humor is merely an irritant: the pastime of those who ever avoid, hiding behind performance, not committing to ideas but rather claiming an ersatz analytic stance centered around *being yourself*. You say what you think, wait for a heartbeat as you read the room, then you smile, say you're kidding. Is that analytic? Hard to make a case for that, I'd say, my face straight for once. I recall a passage from *Portnoy's Complaint* wherein the protagonist is being confronted about his humor: everything he says is twisted to come out "funny," complains his listener. There is something wrong with him. He doesn't want to improve his life. I conjure my analyst saying something like this to me. I hope she hasn't read *Portnoy's Complaint*. Perhaps humor wanes as analysts age, and not because the specter of death is unfunny, necessarily, but rather because age confers authority in our society, and humor and authority are an awkward fit. Authority is less entitled to humor. Again, humor is the tacit right of the underdog, the person whom we cheer on as they disguise their threatening intent to those who are popular or in charge, which may be the same thing. The jester in Lear's court must not offend the master. The comic's "punchline" must bring smiles to an audience; they must entertain as they are "killing it." As candidates assigned to cohorts of learning, we'd regress to a level of middle-schoolish mischief in the comedy club of analytic seminar: invisibly thumbing our noses at times, giving sideways looks, rolling our eyes, sniggering at teachers, an imperturbable institute. Only before the group does the teacher, the titular authority, feel alone and excluded from the joke. This student rebellion is frivolity, acting out, a defense—about as serious as a pratfall. A real joke, as in a truthful, purposeful, analytic jest, is one that doesn't pull its punchline; it stands by the thought that is at the joke's center. It doesn't retreat with a winsome smile or simply mime an action or make itself silly by falling over a prop.

A thought, an idea, that elicits anger makes a person laugh, which is a homonymic cousin to a scoff, sort of twice removed. If the scoff and the laugh are kissing cousins, expressing anger, and if that anger meets with power, then humor is dangerous. It hurts, and therein lies an ethical problem, not just for analysts but for any professional helper. Do no harm. That's our maxim. Break the ice, but don't break living tissue or feelings. In the lives of our patients and in the world they inhabit, there is much to laugh about and not laugh about. So refrain but don't abstain. That quasi-instruction, or exhortation, means something in motion, for there are no prohibitions in psychoanalysis, just as there is no "no" in the unconscious. Psychoanalysis is not that liberating, for there are plenty of don'ts implied via supervision and instruction; but the prohibitions and mandates are mostly contextual, and upon filtering, the don'ts become more like a rough guideline: be careful. The word *depends* comes up a lot, defying the urge to make formula out of instruction. It's tempting to alter this ethos for the sake of feeling governed by something predictable and therefore secure. That may be the ego talking, with one eye on the reality principle. There's much to think about, considering what we should or shouldn't do in the wavy analytic space. And that's the Superego talking, saying "no" and "don't" or "be careful" a lot. The id is also having a say, plus a laugh, saying "go for it," "don't hold back," "let loose," and so on. None of these three units is right per se, at least not all the time.

Much to laugh and not laugh about. Many ideas, opinions, to let loose or hold on to. A patient enters treatment with a few ideas about social phenomena. These ideas: they dribble, leak, or sometimes blast out, depending on what happens in a live moment. Live moment? More live, as in topical, than ever in recent years. A patient is wary of live moments, doesn't want to come to your office, wants telehealth instead. You agree, and right away you are preferable to their boss, who is coaxing them back to the live workplace, ambiguously dangling threats if it doesn't happen. The next patient bristles against all restrictions, has never liked wearing masks, especially not being required to wear a mask. They lost a job because they wouldn't wear a mask, and now they look at you, the prospective helper, an analyst, to see what you'll do and say about that. Someone else says they lost a job because of DEI policies. They were excluded, they say. What do you say, think, about that? Others aren't sure what to think about anything, including identities. Are they transphobic if they don't support transgendered women participating in women's sports? Are they misogynistic if they do? Are they Islamophobic, cosigning genocide, if they don't decry the Israeli government's treatment of Palestinians in Gaza? Are they anti-Semitic if they are critical and signify that belief using words like occupation? Twenty-first-century mores have caught some flat-footed, it seems. A patient listens to what an analyst thinks, scanning for evidence of opinion, experimenting with expression: Can they complain, poke fun at things, observe absurdity? Will you, the analyst, join them, or will you be elusive, a bit like a buoy on the open sea, bobbing along at the surface, not heading anywhere in particular, just floating, acting as a beacon, possibly a cipher, depending on how the patient feels? In response to opinion, protracted diatribes or sporadic remarks, do you sit in nonplussed silence, awkward silence? Or is it another kind of silence: poised and patient, merely waiting for the person's identity, their internal objects, to show amid the opinions?

This may be your analytic identity—one you exude rather than define explicitly with oration. And laughter, or the efforts toward it, will be largely absent during these moments. There may be ice afoot, but it will be a piece to stand on, not break. Not avoid. And opinions will be rarely given, or implied via humor, as neutrality is important: the open space for the patient's ideas, and less so for the analyst, who is not so much the pedagogue in the analytic situation, the open psychological space amid the confined physical space of an office. There may be exceptions, times when an analyst can and perhaps should weigh in on some issue. I did, implicitly at least, with respect to COVID. I stayed away from my office, following the lead of others, the CDC, the institute, who told me to stay away—of my fearful self, who didn't want to die or pass on the possibility of death to a loved one. I lost a few patients (I mean—I think—they left, not died), as many others did, on that particular battlefield wherein the physical space of the office was itself dangerous. On most other matters I am neutral, absorbing many more diatribes than I dish out, except when writing, perhaps. Of course, an analyst can't simply be mute. We aren't garden gnomes. A challenge arrives when it's time to ask that implied question, where are *you*, the "I" that is the subject, in the subject that is a patient/subject's content? This is both a testing ground and a place to pivot, because the patient responding to an internal object may hear a rebuke in the question itself and either take flight or fight. They may split into such dichotomies because thinking doesn't seem possible, hasn't seemed viable in like situations that the unconscious recognizes. The pivot may lie in the analyst taking a stand of sorts: that the live moment in analysis is not one of *those* moments in which the internal object is taking over. The challenge might come in the form of a suggestion that is not a recommendation. It's an observation of a split, a projection, like when an analyst—okay, my analyst—says something like, "Well, that tells us something about how you're taking it," in reference to a challenging question. The suggestion contains an invitation to think about how a mind is working, about the "I" that's present across contexts, the undeniable common denominator that justifies the focus of psychoanalysis: the self. It separates from content, speaks to a continuity of being, and is therefore not locked in temporality. There, that's the stuff of analytic identity, I think, or a semblance of one in progress.

This thing about humor is vexing. On the one hand, it is effortfully peripheral to psychoanalysis, something that, like sex, the patient might feel is there ubiquitously, might get clues of from time to time via the analyst's odd witty remark or an indulgent yet prim smile at a patient's quip. Truth is, like most practitioners of psychoanalysis, I think humor should be restrained, for the most part confined to the polite opening remarks of a presentation or the in-between moments in seminar, to friendly, collegial discussion or the written word that the patient would only read if they googled you diligently. The truth is that I'd sit outside my analyst's office waiting for a session, listening for the faint sounds of conversation, evidence of what she says to others. I was like a jealous husband, and she was like a prostitute, having Johns emerge from her bedroom every 10 minutes from the hour. I'd watch people leave her office—sometimes the same people week to week—and my unconscious would be disabused of the idea that my analyst was exclusive, mine only. And chaste. She wasn't chaste in her humor, I learned, which sparked another layer of jealousy. With me she hardly ever laughed, which I took personally at first—meaning, I thought it meant I wasn't funny—only to rationalize that the absence of laughter was likely a principled stance, an aspect of a committed analytic identity. Well, perhaps not, I once thought when suddenly I heard from the waiting area the unmistakable sound of my analyst's voice dissolving into a loud, joyous-sounding, wall-traversing bray. I couldn't believe it. I didn't want to believe it. My analyst: she was cheating on me with another patient. Worse, I thought: she was cheating on psychoanalysis!

An analyst's identity, my identity, my voice—my *who I am*—is likewise a vexing entity because it is shrouded in mystery, revealing itself sparingly and primarily in the service of another, a patient. The feature of abstinence, so devoutly introduced by Freud, feels feminine, or at least traditionally feminine, despite its espousal for mostly male practitioners by the profession's original patriarch. The analyst privileges abstinence over action, is valued, praised for restraint more so than for an activist or extroverted display. A patient sees their analyst three, four, sometimes five times a week. They spend more time in asymmetrical conversation with this figure than they will with anyone else in their lives, in all likelihood. Perhaps this is why time equals sex in *Catcher*. That's right. Holden asks a schoolmate, Stradlater, if he has given his (Holden's) schoolboy crush, Jane, "the time" in the back of Ed Banky's car. *The time of her life?* Anyway, sex: it's why Holden fears psychoanalysis. Having left sex, some psychoanalysts might now think that time equals parenting, or mentorship, or maybe the "time" of one's life. If retained, the analyst will be more than a commonly reliable figure, solid as a rock, as I thought of that fire chief from *The Towering Inferno*. Akin to other models of constancy and restraint across history and cultures—the priest, the priestess, the monk, the shaman, or the elder—there are the "always there" people whom we seek to adopt or recapture, the secure bases that our parents never were, or never were consistently, or never were perfectly. Likewise, our analysts will sometimes surprise or shock us. Inclusion and exclusion are both real happenings. We will see them four hours per week. That still leaves 164 hours in which they are not there, so to speak. As an analyst, I will surprise and shock sometimes—and sometimes I will mean to do this. Willingly or not, we will dispel illusions of permanence and perfection, or even consistency. I will laugh, whether laughing with or at, or I will be absent, with someone else, being somewhere else, or physically present but *not there* in thought. I will learn to tolerate as well as being tolerated, and at times this may manifest in changed habits, mine included, over seemingly trivial matters in my supposedly nonanalytic daily life. "Are you going to get your coffee cup?" my partner asks, knowing I fret over missing items, moments after reassuring me that she knew its present location, hadn't discarded the cup. "No, it's okay," I reply. "I'm happy to just know where it is."

The cup. The womb. I had a thought, a funny remark, to share with my partner. I didn't for some reason. I restrained, I guess. I didn't mate my impulse to thought. I didn't give it time. Regular time, conscious time, is pressing. I'm in year five of my training. All of my control cases are in their second year or beyond. I am middle-aged, still middle-career, but heading quickly toward its mid- to late stage. Graduation beckons as a finish line, which means it's there for my peers also, especially the hotshots, those pacesetters who streaked ahead, were already immersed in multiple control cases by the end of year one. When we touch base with one another, which is less frequently postseminar, we politely ask where each of us are in the quasi-linear process of training. It would be great if we could all graduate together, we suggest. We could all avoid our Oedipal fears by happily crossing the finish line at the same time, extinguishing competition, achieving a fantasy of equal being. Some of us are writing graduation papers and attending workshops, soliciting mentors, readers, ahead of that endeavor. Mine is about addictions, which I now address as a plurally determined phenomenon, signifying problems that cut across contexts, employing various addictive agents, as they are called, to pursue pleasure, avoid conflict—find omniscient control over guilt and shame, especially shame. Guilt is a postscript, I argue, that which is felt and much expressed in the aftermath of an acting-out binge. It's also a reaction upon a reaction, a breakout from inhibition that results from castration anxiety. And that concept's not as sexist as it seems, I again suggest, though I inhibit a bit of humor when writing of inhibition with respect to men, women, and sex. The outtake reads something like this:

> They are women who are submissive, who behave, and as the bumper sticker reads, they rarely make history. And they are nice guys who finish last, which might mean not winning the race and therefore not getting the girl. Or, one might prefer the phrase to mean gentlemanly postponement, a deference to feminine orgasm.

I felt no shame in writing this, just inhibition based on fear. There were people who would read this and not like it and suggest it get cut, thinking that attempted witticisms have no part in an academic paper, especially one that isn't about analytic identity. So I acted proactively and cut it myself. Shame is the governing feeling with respect to addiction. That's my thesis. It's the feeling least admitted to, the most acted on, I think. More on that later, when I'm writing more about fear, a history of vulnerability, of feeling that.

My cup is full, of something—thoughts of shame displaced by guilt, for example. I am distended with much to think of and do ahead of any kind of finish line: a paper to write; curt rejections from some academic publishers—*We don't think this contributes to analytic literature*; three control cases to continue treating with the help of three different supervisors; reports to complete about each case, plus a statement about my analytic identity, emerging or submerging, or stuck in stasis as it may be. Meanwhile, my personal analysis is bogged down, as in constipated. My mind is full of unrelieved thought, not moving as it should be at this stage of the game. At night, I'm at work, titrating unknowingly. I can feel if not recall dreams, their inchoate scripts and rainbow colors. Then, during the daytime, I hit the treadmill and repeat, feeling diligent and disciplined if dulled and tired. Not enough sleep. But I'm not really tired. I just need to dream more. Actually, I think my dreams have tightly organized, thin scripts with mostly black-and-white backgrounds, some gray or beige hues. Drab and colorless: that's what my analyst says. She also thinks humor is performance, a seeking of good feeling and escape. But you can't liberate a good feeling until you tackle the difficult. That's her thinking too—her aphorism.

"I don't know . . . it all seems to have a kind of lifeless, metallic quality about it." This is a familiar refrain, a typical description by my analyst, of my dreams. Lots of machines in them, it seems. No rainbows, more like tundra grays on uneven landscapes. A lot of numbers too. Doesn't sound flattering, what she hears. My mind sounds like a wasteland. By this point, five years in, analysis is a daily bollocking, as they'd say where I'm from, about where my mind is versus where it would be if it were committed to substance and depth and less so style. At times like this, the wisdom of the tripartite training model comes to me. In the semi-confidential confines of seminar and supervision, you get support as a candidate: teaching, encouragement, gentle criticism maybe. The nutrition is wine and cheese, sweets and salad; the soundtrack is soothing violin strings, a diet of Handel and Bach. Hard rock, streetwise hip-hop, bread and water are reserved for the solitary confinement of training analysis. Here is where you hear that you know nothing about psychoanalysis and might as well start the whole process over again rather than assert knowledge.

But they're my dreams, I rebut. They simply are what they are: me. I think I want some love for my dreams, for my endogenous creativity. I guess I've thought dreams inviolate and deserving of more blessing. No criticism. No "no" imposed on the unconscious. But it's not really a criticism, I rebut to my internal object.

> **She's just observing what's there and what's not. "There's more to it, I think. That's what I remember," I say to her, curtailing an account, after the associations have run dry. "Well, that's what you're aware of," she'll conclude. At least she's not expelling me from the room, telling me to ring the bell when I'm ready—that we'll not speak of it again, this troublesome thing. Next she delivers one of her barbed observations, one I won't mention. I don't want to go into it if you want to know the truth. It staggers me. I'm dazed and shaken. It takes moments for me to find my feet, speak my mind. My first word is not a thought, just a dry utterance. "Uh . . . ," drops unmusically from my lips. I am out of tune, my thoughts dried out.**

Still a long way for me to go, she implies. I envy her, of course. Does she sometimes hate me? I wonder. Putting this thought aside, I imagine she passed the finish line of training years ago. Maybe decades. Being older, she might have other finish lines in mind for all I know. I don't know her. She has her identity, part of which is to not reveal her identity in any biographical sense. She's a screen in that regard—not a blank screen so much as a perfect one in so far as there is little if any reciprocity between us. That's not quite the same as no subjectivity, I think, for we do come up with ideas together at times, that is, shared interpretations. There's a "we" in her vocabulary, I notice. However, she seems free of me, though the reverse doesn't feel true. I feel beholden to her, sensing her impatience with my lack of progress. And despite tension over what I call disagreements and what she calls hostility or lack of awareness, I feel obliged to submit. In that way, she is inside me, a projection that has taken up residency in my head. If there's urgency in psychoanalysis, it's hard to discern it. If there's progress, it's hard to discern it. She has obligations in our arrangement, and she does due diligence in some broadly defined way, and yet I don't feel the strain in her that I feel with my patients. She doesn't complain per se, but neither does she thank me for anything. She doesn't admire me particularly, but neither does she hold me in contempt as far as I can tell. Besides those poles of love and hate, of gratitude or displeasure, I have little evidence of how I impact her. Is this the way to be as an analyst? To be like my analyst, an object of sheer wonder?

This latter reverie represents an important stage of being in one's own psychoanalysis and in training. The experience of wonder conjures an infantile state: one of helplessness, of counteromniscience. Gone is the eagle-eyed scold who found some bravura in the boisterous setting of drug and alcohol treatment, who settled on an idea for a working life shorn of burdensome travel, of heavy lifting. Candidates in training will have adopted numerous identities before contemplating an analytic way of being. All of us have tried on lots of clothes and gazed into mirrors many times before arriving at our institutes. Me. Not me.

That can be me, for a while at least. Definitely not me ever again. These are the thoughts that come to mind, the clothes we tried on and shed. In analysis, the person you are looking at is less readily identifiable because the figure is unclothed by the process. The figure is naked, exhausted, and blinkered—at times a mere gazer, at others an inspired seer with something important to say. The friends and mentors who steer us toward training encourage us to want more, to not run away. They still evince these messages: come back, you Holden wannabe, you longing-to-be-lost-and-then-found child, you otherwise warm and well-fed human being, you punchy rebel, you punched bag. Come back to school. Stay in school. Stay in analysis, find out who you are, don't worry so much about what it will do to you. Meanwhile, keep the day job that has no lifting involved, just heavy listening.

Chapter 5
Vulnerability

I had a morning on the couch yesterday—the dentist couch, that is. I know. Here we go with more stylized humor, featuring a strained analogy between a dental scenario and an analytic situation. It's been done before. It feels like a cliché, like something Holden would have remarked on, dismissed as "phony." Actually, a semi-diligent database search of terms ("dentistry and psychoanalysis") didn't exactly yield a plethora of results from within analytic literature, not that that in itself means this isn't a worthy or well-trodden subject. Indeed, what is a cliché in analytic literature is for an author to open a paper with a chastening claim that his or her subject has been previously neglected within the archives of analytic thought.

My hygienist is really good. She's perky, sometimes a bit jumpy—nervous when first speaking, for example, and giving me darting, averted looks, like she's afraid what she might do to me. Yeah, that's right: what she might do to me. But when she sits down and looms over the gaping oral shaft, she's in her element. When she brings out her tools (now those look like real darts), she's all brisk, no-nonsense movement; she's tidy and sharp, and her gaze is steely and suddenly flush with aplomb. Repression, I guess, with hope in my heart. And me? I am the good patient. Cooperative and sometimes lauded for being so, but my resistance, my unconscious bias against dentistry, shows.

"Turn a bit toward me," she says calmly, unreprovingly, because my anxiety is normal. A moment later, she's back at it, daggering away at a tartar-marred molar. "A bit fluffy," she soon remarks about my plaque-laden front row. I'm nearing periodontal danger, I'm soon informed. My gums are at DEFCON 2, with level 1 being the get-out clause. She takes a picture or two, shows me on her laptop, her evidence-based pronouncement. I figure she'll text me the rest of her photo shoot later, after the appointment, but for now she's pointing out the

worst spots, telling me my teeth aren't happy. Look at that guy, I think, about a bicuspid on my right side. It's leaning backward like it's reaching for cover.

"You know I'm British," I say, trying to inject some fluffy humor to the situation. She returns a thin, indulgent smile, but it's like one of her earlier brisk movements: quick and efficient, then moving on. Her follow-up expression says, *That's no excuse. Besides, the problem's not genetic, though your bruxism may be a function of instinctual drives. But really, this is a developmental issue, the result of a failed nurturing environment.* Jesus, now Winnicott is in my mouth. But I get what she's saying—I need a deep cleaning—and now you will surely get the dental connection: my problems, or my "issues," to borrow a word less defeatist and judgmental, run deep.

We attended a training graduation recently. Is that what it's called, actually? A training graduation? An institute graduation? A psychoanalytic institute graduation? You'll at last qualify when you have learned what it's properly called, someone ought to say. Get your words right. Learn the jargon. And read the room. I didn't read the room. I was in the men's room when something embarrassing happened. No, nothing to do with my teeth or . . . well, I made a faux pas. I was there, at the graduation I mean, to support peers, one or two upperclasspeople who were at training's finish line. At the urinal, which is not the best place for collegial chatter, I saw someone I knew: a supervisor, training analyst; a curriculum committee big shot—someone important in the institute. He shared a first name with someone who had coauthored and published an analytic book recently, which led to my mistake. Right book, wrong author. Congratulations, I said, trying to make friends, make connections. "I think you mean ____," the man replied, smiling kindly. His eyes betrayed his amusement at a candidate who was trying to rub shoulders and getting it wrong. I backed away with something like my tail between my legs and remembered my true purpose for being at the institute that day: that graduation. Oh well, there are worse things that happen in men's rooms.

The analytic thinking, identity: if you decide to give your thoughts spontaneously, directly, without humor being the thing that cuts like a knife—would that constitute an identity? If a patient enters an analyst's office and remarks on its temperature—"It's cold in here"—you can play along, ponder the meaning while remarking on the weather or the suggested inadequacies of your office. Instead, an analyst remarks on the unconscious: "I think you're saying it's cold between us. You've missed me." Cut like a knife? More like cut to the quick. At graduation, a keynote speaker, a local luminary in analytic and medical circles, spoke of institutional history and the waves of conflict that it has survived over the years—going back to the early 1940s in San Francisco. He drew a parallel between the experience of a candidate and that of an institution: both must be flexible, be willing to be vulnerable, take risks. He wasn't joking. Both must accept that inhabiting the analytic space—now that's jargon—means ever not knowing what the real answers are, though if he read this text, he might agree with something I wrote around about the sixth page of chapter 3. He pointed out that once upon a time only medical professionals were accepted by the institute, or the society as it was once called. It was once impervious. This is not unique to San Francisco. He opined that in the era of his training, the 1980s, instruction was more doctrinal, more authoritarian. He seemed to pause on the latter word as if wondering if he was being fair. A touch of sentimental, protective concern maybe. It's interesting to us to observe that even the word *opinion* is subject to revision in recent times. We note the faculty/supervisorial preference for the softer-timbred word *idea*. One has ideas, that represent instincts, but suggesting a moment of creativity, of spontaneity, not something fixed and reified.

We've been here before, the speaker added. He meant that we analysts are resilient, and that the institute is a nurturing parent, however sinister it may seem at times. He spoke of conflicts that have caused divisions, led some to resign from committees and positions of responsibility, others to simply fret in the corner of their offices or in silos of like-minded thought. We go to war, or rather we genteelly skirmish, and upon someone's victory, we multiply. As in that Winnicott anecdote that is retold ad nauseum, we drop thought bombs and let the mic drop, and then we boom, so to speak, with new babies, recruits for an altered Superego of the future. It's clear that many have opinions, not just ideas, about the direction of the institute, of the psychoanalytic movement. What's not clear are the specifics, because unless one is a member of the committee or ensconced in one of those silos, you'll only hear the basics, which means the allusions to conflict, not the play-by-play, the knotty details. And it's not just graduation ceremonies that skirt the issues. It's other semipublic settings, like classrooms, case conferences, possibly supervision hours, analytic hours: in each of these forums, private and not, an ethos of nonintrusion seems to prevail, as in don't intrude on a candidate's experience, don't contaminate the analysand's hour with the stuckness of opinion. The ambience of disquiet, navigated by reticent caretaking, permeates an institute, stirring disappointment. Is psychoanalysis really so special, special enough that its players would fare better with conflict than average members of society?

Perhaps not, we consider. At a distance or at close quarters, we notice that communication breaks down and that bad object experiences explode, leading to evacuations, splitting. Someone's opinion is rejected by an ambiguously dominating faction in a group, and so they leave, sulking and disconsolate. Or they recruit an ally or two, craft a letter of protest, and either effect a coup in the night or a jailbreak. Over the next few days, there may be emails spreading the news; a newsletter announcement may follow at a later date. Some disagreement is approached, then circumvented, zeroed in on, but then pushed back. Or else a retreat occurs, or the noise of clashing voices dissolves the substance, culminating in morbid impasse. We've seen it in cohort disputes, in candidate-wide discussions. These events become urban legends. Gatherings of peers aimed at resolving intragroup tension or exploring issues relating to diversity, exclusion and inclusion, have deteriorated into scapegoating rancor and blocked expression. As candidates, we prefer as ever to blame authority, the teachers and administrators. They are the parents of our training who have let us down, having failed in their nurturing role. We dare not risk ostracism from our siblings, our secret competitors. As a result, we haven't gotten very far in our peer-centric discussions, which is to be expected given the weight of problems and the awkward frameworks that are devised for our meetings. Yes, so little time afforded, so little space. These are excuses, says an average view; reality resistance may be the analytic take—some things are indeed true but still limited as explanations, ignoring that ever elusive something else that is not named. Not even here in cloistered text. The problem is we think we've come a long way to even be here in psychoanalytic training, so we figured the problem-solving, the creative, cooperative thinking, ought to have been made easier.

Actually, it's harder. It's harder because we pause and think. Contrarily, that might mean equivocation, which connotes passivity, lack of conviction, because in these moments we feel alone. Otherwise, it suggests open-mindedness, a willingness to explore rather than jump quickly to what is presumed to be true, what someone insists is true. We are familiar with those moments when someone in a crowd says how things are to the crowd and then nods, affirming the self-evidence of their thought, hoping for agreement, ready to withdraw if not. We wonder if they feel alone and vulnerable sticking their necks out like that. We suppose that if paused decision and exploration is indeed a virtue, then at least something ought to be said that speaks to the, uh, idea? Yes, we've been here before, we again suppose. It's a repetition. Tower (1956) offers the idea that countertransference, in contrast with, say, empathy, is based on repetition compulsion. Maroda (2022) suggests that enactments, which proceed from countertransference, are borne of passivity in the treatment. Passivity in the treatment, and also at an institution, in the life of a candidate. Sitting on the sidelines, waiting, watching, scratching one's chin and listening with an inscrutable air.

This brings to mind again the issue of neutrality, which I've come to think is about leaving space for patients' thoughts, not preempting or influencing their opinions with our own. That's more or less what I've thought all along—I mean, since I first decided to train as a clinician, not form an analytic identity per se.

Anyway, it's not about silence in the face of injustice. Such conceptions aren't even at the heart of the matter. Agitated candidates, psychoanalytic community members, the public at large, do not think that psychoanalysis is indifferent to, say, racism, because not enough analysts either present or write about the problem of racism. Nor do they form their impressions of analytic thinkers simply because of media caricatures, or because they have magically listened in on countless exchanges between analysts and their patients and determined that analysts are not validating rightful complaints in numbers. No, people think psychoanalysis is racist because of other numbers, as in not enough numbers of people of color being represented at analytic training institutes or within psychoanalytic associations. They're saying, look around, in your meetings, in your offices and waiting areas. See who's there and who isn't, in numbers. Hello, this is your 2020 air-raid warning!

At times, we might remember the personal antecedents of our passivity, especially those of us who have siblings. We remember lounging in a living room, sparring tensely, figuring each other out, seizing the moments to get what we want or else miss out and watch as that bolder sibling takes away the family goods. And the parents? They didn't help. At the decisive moment, they had gone to bed, tired, thinking of something else and leaving us to our own devices. When we ask them to intervene, to issue a decree over conflicts and save us, they reluctantly and therefore carelessly strike the gavel, choosing arbitrarily who won or lost. We remember, and we repeat. And maybe our fellow candidates, our analytic peers, and also our patients will show us the way if we can't remember but still repeat, if we can't decide or act.

I had to decide some things with a patient or two. Susan thought that I wasn't tracking her very well and said so. I wasn't keeping up with the details, was transposing names and places, making mistakes in listening. Mistakes in listening: a good title for something, I think. Maybe I was overworked, Susan suggested, which meant that she didn't have my undivided attention. How true. How exposing. I am exhausted by the anaclitic needs of some patients and left abandoned by the ghosting habits of others. I may have scratched my chin and listened with an inscrutable air; I can't quite remember. I don't really want to. I prefer to think that I made an apt interpretation at this point: something that reflected the importance of my being there for her and the disappointment she'd feel if I wasn't. A bad object experience. A necessary feature of an analytic experience, I may have thought, which will have felt better. Possibly a secret graduation requirement. Must make a note of this moment and present it to my supervisor or include it in my next case report. I gathered my wits soon thereafter and refocused: yes, she is important,

and I am important to her, but this problem requires thinking, which I should not confuse with equivocation. I am reminded of her conflicts: she wants guidance and not imposition. She wants me to think with her, not for her. She wants a mastery of something not done properly once upon a time: she moves away from the object, who observes the omnipotent flourish on shaky legs but does not intrude, either rescuing from failure or thwarting a growth moment. In the present, I am not meant to decide anything per se, only point out potential flaws, inconsistencies, tell her when she *might* make a mistake. This requires me to follow along diligently, not lose track. At a glance, it doesn't seem like such a heavy task, but even if I do this well for a single patient per day versus seven or eight, it is. It is.

Meanwhile, Joe, another control case, was threatening to leave. Actually, he wasn't threatening to leave. He was threatening to reduce his commitment to analysis to one or two meetings per week, which is tantamount to leaving when you're a candidate and you're in a numbers game. Thinking of it that way is my problem. It's not something Joe does, this intemperate pullout. He's not one of those patients with a volatile relationship history or a checkered employment record. Again I caught myself thinking something that wasn't useful in the moment. There I was thinking of what this wasn't, not what it was. What was happening? Joe reminded me that it—meaning his desire to cut back—had been happening for some time and then implied that I hadn't said anything about it. I hadn't decided for him, issued a decree. I hadn't stepped up as an authority, a nurturing parent, and guided him in his decision. With Joe, the turnaround from compliance to rebellion would have been protracted and then impulsive. He might have missed a session or two and blamed it on a family conflict. He will have forgotten to bring a check, perhaps thinking that I wasn't doing my job and therefore not deserving payment. He would have come late to my office and blamed it on the traffic on the 242. Actually, he has come late to my office and blamed it on the traffic on the 242. His resistance is a slow burn, not the live bristling wire that Susan presents. So he did what he's been doing for years, for his entire lifetime, perhaps. He acted. He acted out, to be more precise, having stopped thinking about what his desire to reduce frequency of sessions was all about—only that he was tired and he wanted to do other things, like play with his kids more. So disappointing, I will have thought, thinking of myself before him. I got to that afterward. How long had he been in analysis? And how bad a job had I been doing that he was still thinking, or not thinking, like this?

Freud, on beginning treatment (1913), had made this seem simpler somehow, for that's when technique was evolving, with the "project" of psychoanalysis still in early development. In that burgeoning model, the analyst does not requ unconditional acceptance from a patient. No faith in a cure per se is required. In this way, Freud scolded religion even as he mimicked some of its norms. You take on a patient for a couple of weeks, perhaps more, and then take it from there. If the patient is a friend, said friend and the analyst should be prepared to lose that friendship for the sake of the treatment. That seems strange to read today—seems like that would have been a given, not worth saying. Maybe that insinuation of scientific objectivity should have gone without saying. That said, should anything go without saying, we might wonder? The patient is advised to be critical, even suspicious of the treatment process. Apparently, Freud wished to dispel an impression that psychoanalysis should be authoritative, relying on a devout adherence to an analyst's framework and interpretations. Next, Freud outlined the structure, those reified details pertaining to frequency of visits or duration of treatment, the use of a couch wherein patient and clinician don't even look at each other. Six days a week, he also advised, asserting a preference as much as a prescription. These hours are leased by patients, and they are liable for them, Freud added. As to duration, he was philosophical or rather mythological. He quoted a philosopher from Aesop's fables who directed a man to walk in answer to a query about how long a walking journey should take. The philosopher reasoned he couldn't know the answer until he had observed the man's stride.

Psychoanalysis is always a matter of long periods of time, half or whole years—certainly longer than what a patient expects. That's what Freud suggested, anyway, and there are surely candidates who will expect this degree of innocence. When a patient asks about duration of treatment, ostensibly so they might structure their lives, inform their loved ones, and set up the weekly structure, we gulp and then solemnly outline the recommendation. We know not what we're getting ourselves or them into. When we're lucky, or not depending on what we think we're getting into, we have a patient who has been here before, or they've read something we have read and therefore have come to know what's on offer. "When can we move to four times per week?" this person asks, seemingly eager for analysis. Freud didn't seem to expect this level of determination. He observed resistance or expectation of quick results. Cure me of my headaches, and so on. So tell patients ahead of time that psychoanalysis is a long process, an indeterminate one at least. Change is slow. The unconscious is timeless, and treatment sets in motion a complex process, replete with obstacles. The patient who doesn't accept this precautionary word is likely not suitable for treatment, but it's better to give some semblance of a prediction lest patients say they've been duped at some later point. You don't want those "You never said . . . " expressions to emerge, especially if money becomes the problem—the *issue*. Money, like sex, is dirty and therefore subject to prudishness and shame. False shame, we might add.

This is why we're supposed to shed inhibitions, eschew philanthropic illusions, and assert a just fee for our time. Time: it's our only commodity in strictly economic terms. We might consider the class implications, our place in the economic superstructure, for there is no surplus value in psychoanalytic work, or passive income; we make an income off no one's labor but our own, and we make no commission from a patient's improved mental condition. There are no late fees for services unpaid, no interest upon outstanding debts. The deadness of a plateau and the magic of a breakthrough both cost the same. Anyway, better to assert claims for our time than to offer a free service and expect gratitude, or fear demands for refunds. Free treatment would increase resistance, Freud thought, though he toyed with and then toiled on the idea of free clinic services. There may have been a Marxist or two in earshot at the time—someone like Wilhelm Reich, maybe, or Fromm or Horney—who helped devise clinics that provided free outpatient mental services across 10 cities in Europe during the 1920s and '30s (Danto, 2007).

Regardless, this is a matter that surely changes with the times. Once, it may have seemed that a middle-class income would be sufficient to gird a living plus the indulgence of an analytic treatment. Would this be true of an average Millennial or a so-called Gen Z today? Only at a significantly reduced fee, we're inclined to think. It treads a fine line, this setting of expectations. Unless the patient is a liberally educated intellectual, an urban-dwelling denizen in all likelihood, or born into a family of psychoanalysts, or all of the above, they are likely to be as skeptical of psychoanalysis as Freud expected, plus some. If you tell them that you expect attendance at sessions multiple times per week in order for treatment to be effective, patients might think you exploitative, or else they will have friends and family who will say so. They'll google their options, consider microdosing psychedelic drugs instead. Why is psychoanalysis necessary? Well, again, because change is slow, because resistance is ubiquitous and powerful, even if interventions, like the "you miss me" comment, are decisive and reaching. The habits of day-to-day conscious and unconscious life will still outnumber all those hours on a couch; they'll fight hard with those four or more hours per week, we say.

So the patient will see the analyst more days per week than they won't. That's meaningful. Initially, the polemic that introduces treatment may center on that antiresistance idea, the seeming cure that is repetition but not rinse. But soon it will seem that something else is being offered—something more change inducing, more threatening and yet rich and wholesome at once: a relationship in which two people don't sleep together but become closer than they ever thought they would to another human being. It's intense, we're told in early training, whether we've experienced this firsthand or not, from the couch and not just from behind it. Incidentally, that couch signifies that we won't be "seen" in the literal sense, or "seeing" our patients more times per week than not. The fleeting glance exchanged at the door may be the most we'll take in visually of our patients or our own analyst. This privileging of the couch may enable the hypnotic remnant, as Freud thought. Or, as contemporary supervisors seem to agree, the couch elicits the internal experience, the dropping into a dream recollection or deeper state of mind. It surprises us that less is said of the sexual dampening, or contrarily, of the excitation, for it may be reasonable to imagine that the couch's other purpose is to thwart an objectifying gaze or else stir fantasy. The couch versus the "sit-up" position: "It stops us from looking at women's breasts," said one candidate who now lives in muted ignominy. So did Zoom, we might have replied, dodging an ethical point. Maybe other points also. After all, Zoom will have seemed unanalytic for several reasons, not least of which that it forces us to meet each other's gaze while concealing our hands. The author of the quip tried to walk back any offense, saying, "It enables thinking when we look away." The audience returned pale smiles, thinking it was too late to get the sex out of our minds that we thought had been put in.

Whether telehealth is more erotic or perverse than the couch could be the subject of a separate paper or book entirely. Writing a year ahead of the COVID lockdown, Ehrlich (2019) cited research indicating that telehealth had already found traction in analytic practices by the time of his writing. He reviewed the opinions of some analysts/authors who bemoaned its encroachment on the grounds that telehealth unduly accommodates patients and thwarts patient imagination; he then cast telehealth as a scapegoat. It's a hypothesis, not a fact, that use of a computer screen compromises right-brain function in both clinician and patient (Schore, 2011). Ultimately, we can't blame technology for our forgetting, our lapses in concentration, our lack of attunement. Or our unwillingness to congregate, we might add. Zoom compresses space, protested one candidate in training, makes them feel trapped and stared at. We have certainly heard of an opposing view aimed at a more traditional psychoanalytic totem, the couch. The couch provokes erotic fantasy by situating analyst and analysand in seductive positions: one seated and peering forward at a downward trajectory from behind; the other laying down, looking upward or inward, but tempted to look over a shoulder to peek at the listener. Would an intersubjective or relational analyst, so called, inch their chairs forward to allow visual contact from a sideways-looking patient? Would they think this an egalitarian gesture, a token of increased presence within a still asymmetrical arrangement? It is perhaps a matter of debate whether the seated or the laid-down figure is the more seductive, but we think average opinion would posit the analyst as the more powerfully positioned and the supinely situated patient as more vulnerable. Indeed, some of our patients have said as much. They feel fidgety and tense, and not just because our couches tend toward firm severity versus cushiony softness. Perhaps it's that remnant of hypnosis, as Freud suggested. When we're on our backs, we're preparing to sleep, to go unconscious and dream, which is conducive to analytic method, of course, but it also conjures risk at the hands of a predator and forces us to trust any figure that will loom over us. Or not, if we are let off that particular psychoanalytic hook.

That charmless remark from that candidate about not looking at women's breasts was more than a burst of puerility followed by a scrambling save. It felt like a locker room jibe: an anachronistic poke at authority, an echo of a male-dominated workplace, something that ought to have changed, as in left the building by now. But it was also a sideswipe at peer sensibilities or demographic assumptions. The source of the remark was a woman, which may surprise given the masculine whiff of the joke. That element appeared to still the judgment of listeners: a small handful, a carefully if spontaneously selected group for humor that has a limited constituency. Whether the joke's author knew it or not, we were meant to think about the different layers. We could be naughty children, toying with the sanctity of psychoanalytic icons during our breaks, but not break a silver-sprinkled rule that you can make fun of anyone, even a reader, except someone who may be in front of you. Over coffee or at the watercooler, or between the fundraising host's wine and cheese, we could be careless with our antisocial and outdated thoughts and risk rebuke from a largely progressive peer base. Or we could learn that mischievous impulses might come from unlikely or unforeseen sources and therefore be stopped in our thought tracks. Perhaps the breast joke was ironic, a parody of a moment from the institutional past, told to remind us of something uncomfortable that lingers. We didn't dare ask. We dare to blame or rescue with our thought about it. So there's something to consider. The classroom and the playground still have a locker room attached; it's just that the locker room has gotten bigger, and more—that qualitative and quantitative "more" that we're ever saying we want more of—have been invited into the locker room, and sometimes someone says something that lets us know that some things haven't changed.

Sometimes candidates joke about the changes that might happen or that are happening elsewhere but haven't yet happened at our institutions. Take the tiresome frequency issue, for example.[1] We might agree that it's time to reduce the requirement of a four- or five-times-per-week analysis to a three-times-per-week analysis. It's subjective, we may argue. It's not like when a dental hygienist tells you that your gums ought to be at three or four millimeters from the crown of the tooth versus an unhealthy five millimeters or a dreaded six millimeters. The fire chief Steve McQueen of their world, that professional person, is enviably without doubt that the farther down the gumline goes, the worse the matter is for the patient: the deeper the tissue, the deeper the disease, and the discoloration of the pink surface will be further evidence of rot. But analytic candidates and their mentors can think differently, more flexibly, about the matter of numbers and psychoanalytic rot: whether that fourth session of the week is a tipping point after which a discernible change is afoot. We can think on the matter, even dwell on it indefinitely, but patients like Joe are querulous and skeptical. They are wondering, making a consumer's judgment, reverently or not, about whether this "more" is all it's cracked up to be. Where's the joke? Well, it's at that coffee shop or watercooler again. It's in another quip, this one more obviously aggressive and rivalrous than sexual. Yes, the candidates that follow us in our footsteps may someday be let off another hook—we mean graduate—with cases of three sessions per week instead of four or five. But can we agree that those of us who did that extra, the over-the-top sessions, worked a little harder, that we're better analysts than thou who did less?

No. That would be the ill-humored and blunt response. Or not necessarily—that's the addendum of choice for a hedged bet. It won't be so simple as that. In response, we'd be quietly truculent like elders who envy change, hoarily moaning that when they went to school they had to walk through sleet and snow, uphill, in both directions. The expanded retort of our candidate issue might suggest that little is made more difficult or worthy simply by an added hour of labor per week. One might as well ask how many hours per week are required for parenthood. It's a not-so-wild comparison. Philips (1995) suggests that an analyst has to fall into the trap of being treated like a parent—an authority of sorts—and then refuse to be one. The child and later patient expects expertise, knowledge, from the elder. They might not expect to understand this knowledge and may be cowed by it. Holden remarked on this kind of expert knowledge, saying, "All you have to do is say something nobody understands and they'll do practically anything you want them to." For him, the pretense of expertise enabled power and distance. For our consideration, the analyst is an expert to the patient's conscious mind, the holder of a secret that may be shared if the subject is worthy. And you don't get this secret just because you've paid for it, though you might get it if you try harder, put in more hours, do the legwork, or click a lot if what you did was spend much of your training in front of a monitor. As candidates, we're trained to offer interpretations, not to impart knowledge. Knowledge isn't necessarily good, Freud suggested, thinking the pursuit of knowledge a Faustian hole. So we are shepherding a search for a secret, aiming words at what is missing in a patient's thoughts and leaving something out from our own. We hold back something we think but don't really know, frustrating that patient who senses that reticence in us, and possibly complains because they want to know what they think we know. Rationally, they know they're meant to figure out problems and other truths for themselves, to do the work that analysts suggest is there to do. However, even to suggest this to them is to act like one knows something, that we are experts on mental health, and that patients are meant to follow our lead in taking the lead. Our lead into what? What are we telling them? *You start*: that roughly captures an analytic opening to a session. What if we're not so much telling patients anything or imparting education as listening. Just listening. And in that listening is a multilayered task, the work of being available to absorb and allow countless repetitions, to satisfy with listening and leaving space, but also dissatisfy by withholding and exposing a vacuum.

It's a state of vulnerability to act like an expert of something undefined yet beg off explanation of anything specific. It's harder still to go to work each day and act like we are worthy of being paid for all this withholding of information, this mere listening interspersed with observations that keep thought going but don't provide or destroy with finality. And if it's hard for a seasoned analyst to pull this off, it's surely harder still for candidates who can't even tell their patients—not yet anyway—that they've arrived at the point wherein they can call themselves analysts. We barely know what we're doing in a profession built on authority. We're not yet and never will be experts in any conventional sense, soothing or terrorizing with expert knowledge. We can be fired for acting like we do. We can be hired, fired, rehired, sort of, have the sessions reduced, have them canceled or ignored for not being the good enough expert or replacement parent that patients don't know they're looking for. Conceivably, we can be sued, depending on what we promise. How do we exist in a material world on this basis? It's not as though we can market the qualities of an analyst beyond what is teasingly known: that we listen better than most, better than thou. Perhaps, hopefully and not, this listening, plus the reveries we share that nudge patient thoughts along, has been so scarcely offered that it is as unique as it has ever seemed—and will continue to be coveted. That's kind of what we market: we do something rare, and among other things, we think our task is secure because we don't imagine that AI will be able to do what we do anytime soon.

We hope not. We hope because we don't know what robots can do any more than we know what human beings can do. We've had to consider this issue when we entered analysis ourselves and later when we were selecting candidates, or when they pursued us, prodded by longing, plus a referral. Did they choose us, or did we choose them? Did we choose analysis? It's a fair question to ask couples, so why not analysts and analysands: Who initiated this arrangement? Who asked who to go out on that first date? Back to the first question: How do we know if a patient can do analysis, or if we have what it takes to be an analyst for any patient, whether they are beseechingly interested, diffidently present, or—as often seems the case—cautiously detached and oblique in most of their expressions? The point is that patients make us work hard, whether they seem motivated for care or not, but only if we're able and willing to think about whatever face they present. We can do some reading on this subject, check out what Coltart (1987), for example, researched on the matter of patient suitability: whether an individual can (in an early interview) exhibit capacity for self-reflection at a distance from emotional experience, bring forth memories that associate, discuss uncomfortable feeling states across contexts, use imagination to recognize an unconscious mental life. A tall task—not one for just a single interview of course. This matter also brings to mind the caveats of supervisors and analysts, who vary in the way they present: some are warm and effusive in their support of a fledgling analyst, while others are coolly testing, as much protective of an institute or of analytic tradition as concerned with the plight of any given candidate. This type will offer cryptic provocations like, "You know, you can't ask someone to do the work you haven't done yourself."

Ostensibly, this is a chastisement but also a challenge. The recipient of the sting is meant to seize the moment and think—think about what's missing in the work with a patient, what's important in the work with the patient. For some, it would be tempting to give up when faced with this kind of rebuke. It's a not-good-enough moment, for sure. That's how it feels, anyway. It's even reminiscent of moments outside of analytic training, or moments that previously signaled inclusion or else rejection, feeling like a closed door or possibly a call for perseverance. The closed-door examples associate to closed-society thinking, closed minds. It's like a stiff arm from a 12-step old-timer who says that only fellow recovering addicts can help one another. It's like an inflammatory post on a Listserve that addresses a must-answer political question du jour and laments the inhumanity of organizations if they don't mirror concerns. It's like a question from a patient who has just fielded a challenging thought from their analyst, so they counter defensively, ask something like, "Do you have kids?" or "Have you ever been to . . . ?" to centerpiece credentialing, force divides, and deflect from a painful subject. Pause. As would-be analysts, we can linger on these moments of projection amid discomfort. We can practice reverie before or even as we move on, listening and thinking still. "Have you ever been to the bottom of the ocean?" you wonder—metaphors now (excuse me again) flooding into mental space. Have you ever gone deep, or does the dream keep stopping when the water turns black?

Snap out of it, says the ego. Snap back into it, says the unconscious, equally willful. Maybe the patient does so before you. Maybe they do so in the moments after they've rebuked an analyst's interpretation, after they've reasserted the hegemony of their reality resistance.

A doctor details the circumstances of what he calls a botched operation. The patient—his patient—lived, but the recovery wasn't perfect. There were lingering symptoms, an unforeseen outcome. The doctor is dissatisfied, self-critical, and stiffly resistant to my suppositions. It is hard for him to accept that he cannot

control what happens, that he can't predict every outcome. He should have done better, he insists. He knows better, certainly better than me, he implies. Then, in the silence of that stuck place, his eyes become glassy, like he's drifting off, having another kind of thought. Loss. His mind has wandered onto an idea about why he became a doctor in the first place. He wanted to help people, to save lives. He briefly chuckles, sneers even, at his trite desire. But he holds on to some piece of the thought—this thing about loss. "I could lose," he utters. He could lose people, as in his patients, but also his loved ones. He had lost loved ones. And it didn't have to be that way. Now it's about tragedy. He idly muses about tragedy and shakes his head, adding that there's something important, by which he means terribly motivating, about the tragedy of loss. Life has meaning because we can lose it, he decrees. Nothing lasts. Then he chides himself once again for his self-indulgence.

It's not easy to know, or to learn to know, when a patient is in defense—being "self-indulgent," as this patient pronounced—versus being in some alternative mental place, thinking openly, exploratively, using that requisite imagination that Coltart pinged as a criterion for psychoanalytic treatment. From the couch it's easier to tell, we'd suggest, when our analysts seem to think that we're using our minds analytically, that we're doing *the work*. We can tell because they've stopped talking or, more precisely, because they've stopped interrupting us, telling us that our thoughts have drifted from something important to something diffuse, diluted, and therefore evasive. Those who haven't experienced this kind of interaction in analysis might consider themselves lucky, for it is jolting to be interrupted midthought and to be told, by implication at least, that the thought previously in progress was off base in terms of analytic progress. Or perhaps we are lucky to experience this brand of active listening versus the treatment of a more superficially patient and quietist listener. But we wonder if the former paradigm of an active, challenging, thought-interrupting analyst was ever thus, at least within the context of candidate training. Operating from the premise that a would-be analyst needs to do the work if they are to facilitate the work with their own patients, might a training analyst be more assertive, more urgent in their task?

Would they be on top of so-called reality resistances, interrupt when that doctor plods through the details of what he called a botched operation? Would our analysts have thought the reverie about loss a self-indulgence, a getting away from something else that was important or more important? Imagine a dialogue between a training analyst and analysand from, say, 80 years ago, roughly. In London:

"Now, see that you've shifted again, your attention. It's difficult for you to stay with an idea, which leaves everything sort of . . . watered down."

"No, look. Really, there *is* an air-raid warning. Don't you hear that?"

"Yes, it is happening, but it's not the only thing that's happening here. Donald, we've heard this before from you and it seems like a go-to for you. Now, St. Paul's is fine. Paddington Green is fine. Homes are being destroyed—that's true—but what we're missing here is the blitz that's happening inside you."

The blitz is inside me? An average patient might repeat the words, negotiating their entry to the mind. For a moment at least, the thought pauses, competes against nothing coming from within because it—the analyst's interpretation—has not previously been thought about. Or it has been forgotten. We get away from something important, become passive as analysands, analysts. Yes, you can't do the work of analysis if you haven't done the work of analysis. The hungry candidate thinks of both sides of this divide, feeling like an inhabitant of both positions. We eye graduation, having attended the rites granted our elder classmen and classwomen. Those were happy occasions, suggestive of belonging, warm oceanic feelings for years to come. As a not-yet-there figure, you feel yourself wading in cooler waters still, at an uncertain depth, untethered from something secure on the surface. Borrowing from transient headlines from the summer of 2023, you wonder if your descent is like that of a portly submersible—an atom-bomb-sized submarine that has drifted from its course, dropping like a falling stone and being crushed in an instant for having taken on too much weight, all because a legendary relic lying dormant on the floor of the North Atlantic was worth looking at. This is a catastrophe, but your thought is different—a catastrophizing—because, as either your analyst or supervisors or all will remind you, your thought is neither action nor material reality. It is a dream.

It's just a thought, the desire, or fear. Candidates begin training and they want more. They find themselves submerged halfway, and they want to stop or take a break. Seminar ends. Attention turns to control cases, the writing of a paper. More analysis, less time spent with candidate peers in a structured environment. Change. If you want more, conflict or siloed like-mindedness, you'll have to go for it; it won't come to you. Everything seems to change, and the transitions feel chilly, like cold water.

Susan had felt untethered by my losing track. As I recovered my grip, I followed her better, kept my mind open, my hands figuratively free lest she fall off from a thought. *You're getting away from something important*: it's a useful phrase. Think

I'll keep using it. She keeps coming back, wanting more. No worries here about lapsed attendance, the falling numbers of analysis. She's into me and I'm into her. In vernacular, as at deep sea, it's called a crush.

Joe is losing the thread, forgetting more details about his day-to-day life and losing track of himself in analysis. Meanwhile, I'm losing my grip and missing him already, even though we keep seeing each other. I miss him more than he seems to miss me. That wasn't supposed to happen. It's a countertransference response that I'm meant to take into my own analysis and examine, possibly expunge. Or no—not expunge—better understand. That's it. Mustn't lose track of my purpose, or catastrophize. But it does hurt, or feel uncomfortable, this chilling water. He wants away, has other things to do, he says. His crush is over—so he thinks. Twice per week versus four times per week: who knew that numbers would matter so much. So little time! But he's made his decision, differentiating from the authority that is me, though he's not quite putting it like that. He says it feels like growth, and he may be right about this: his wish to not adhere to the framework recommended to him by his analyst is a shift from an old pattern. Not long ago he associated to his childhood school days. He spoke about skipping school and telling lies about it, unaware that he was foreshadowing his analytic rebellion. Once upon a time, lying brought shame, though it would feel good initially. Had Joe felt like me, he might have thought of Holden. He skipped school and more. He ran away from Pencey, dashed off to New York, though he kept in touch with a teacher or two. He even visited one, then he dashed away again, thinking his kindly host a sexual predator. Yeah, what will they do to you? Instead, Joe had another character in mind, a real kid's story. He felt like Pinocchio living without strings, skipping class and hanging out with bad kids, doing what he wanted, but not using expertise to get his way—only to hold secrets and tell lies. It even felt good to tell lies, to pull the wool over the adult gaze, feel at once big and small, to feel big and free as his, uh, nose grew.

In training, our noses are growing, taking on more but exposing us with their growth. We've had aha moments. Mine have encircled feelings of shame and guilt, in that order. I think of shame first because it comes first, is older developmentally: the preverbal, pre-Oedipal experience of being small, weak, being bad and exposed as such in front of a judge. Freud (1905, 1917, 1923) wrote that a child internalizes this judge, develops a Superego, and learns to feel bad about action and thought, not just fear judgment and punishment. We have patients who feel small and aggrandize themselves, squashing shame and replacing it with guilt. Or we have patients whose pattern is to feel small or to make themselves small and humble, in seeming inhibition of grandiose states that would in turn lead to guilt. In our offices, within cabinets, we'll have stacks of notebooks by now, filled with the verbatim process notes, furiously scribbled over years, representing an inchoate record of these kinds of observations. It wouldn't make for good reading, even that which can be transcribed. As time passes, each note of each session takes on a more obscure, distant quality. The sessions these notes capture become more difficult to remember, revealing the limits of symbolic tracking.

Invoking the Bionian cliché of no memory or desire, we should gather together all of our notebooks of process notes and create a bonfire. Let them burn. Or, since some of us are in California, which has banned bonfires for generations, and living in the 21st century with climate change tipping points beckoning, we should recycle the paper of our notebooks instead. Our colleagues in Portugal and elsewhere should do the same. Forget the words, save the world. I don't know if bonfires are allowed in Portugal. Much is allowed out there, my friend Pedro suggests. His country is freer, he implies, if more impoverished. Does that limit freedom? Well, I'm not paying for it, I crudely rebut. On the Algarve Coast, you can build shaky looking, misshapen homes and fix them precariously on shallow cliffs. Haughty Spaniard tourists or ogling Anglos scoff at the dereliction, envy deregulation, the free infrastructure, but the local mafia is in charge, say the reliably informed. Apparently, they don't mind disorder, dangerous living. Down here you're on your own, says the ambience, the fantasy projected onto the sunbaked, rugged landscape. The nudity on the public beaches is also striking, breaking no one's rules, it seems, just stirring fantasy. Psychoanalysis has a place in this culture, making it less repressive, maybe. We wonder what psychoanalysts get away with in this milieu.

In the postseminar drift, we continue on with our psychoanalytic project. We go to our workshops, write our papers. I wrote mine in a binge of postseminar inspiration. A rough draft was done in a month. The sculpting of the presentation was more painstaking and protracted. Its later dissemination brought laudatory support, a touch of hauteur to my self-image. Attempts at publication elsewhere are more chastening, bring me down to earth again. Patronized for my worthy intentions, I've been critiqued for shoehorning Freud into the subject of addiction while a case illustration serves up narcissistic wounding as the root of problems. Reconcile contrary theories. Decide on a direction and stick with it. Write as if history matters, but recognize where theories have shifted. Integrate! Reviewers might think that AI would do a better job.

I keep going to my analysis, ever working on myself, thinking and dreaming—daydreaming, sometimes real dreaming. It never seems to stop, this lifestyle. I'm not shocked by this observation. Actually, very little about psychoanalysis has been shocking. Maybe that's because I haven't changed much. The bingo or aha interpretations: I never was prone to those. Away from my office, I have bingo moments, thought orgasms that give me a kick on a morning jog. They bring transient relief from the unpleasure of not knowing things. Back at the office, I've become more succinct with my insights, perhaps, more adroitly to the point on what I think is happening and why. Less verbose. I follow a flow of a session, tolerate ambiguity, including stretches when I'm not sure what's happening, except between myself and my analysands: Are we close or not so much? I relax. The evenly hovering attention: yeah, it floats all right, but our heads are not always above water. Something will come, like a link to a previous thought and to a not-quite-bingo surprise. The thought establishes contact with the unconscious, sort of slipping into it. Well into the analysis, the patient might reveal something they haven't before and also think about the prior withholding. We may notice together that something has changed, the relationship. A kind of love has happened in these meetings of ours. What we speak of and how we do it now feels indispensable.

Like other candidates, I'll dip my toes into the teachers' pool, volunteer at a satellite program sponsored by our institutes, adopt the vain desire to become a well-known thinker, a budding theoretician. In a class designed for a six- or eight-week stint, we'll spread the word about full psychoanalytic training to students of various ages and backgrounds. Some are doctors, steeped in science, well-bred in evidence-based practice. Like the social workers and therapists, they come fresh from their clinics and community mental health centers, their half-hour to 40-minute "check ins" with oft-suicidal and otherwise disorganized patients, people who may or may not be hospitalized before the workday's over. These students will be curious at least about analytic training, about theory and method, and be variably eager to give it all a shot, see how it might apply to their working worlds. Some will be in their own analyses already and evaluating options, where they are in their careers, their lives. "How long does it last?" they'll ask of this thing. "How much does it cost? What do you actually have to do, to accomplish, in order to graduate, to become a psychoanalyst?" And lastly, beyond the numbers and procedure, "What do you actually learn?" The conversation might get to that last bit, but maybe not, because the numbers are a daunting hurdle. We'd offer our experience, be honest about it all, the concrete details and the unknown, the uncertainties. At some point, we'd pause before asking if they want to apply for full analytic training. We'll chuckle perhaps but then keep our faces straight as theirs say things like, "Oh, hell no!" or "Is this a joke?"

One thing we don't offer, because we don't know, is a view on how much psychoanalysis we'll even get to practice in the future. We don't know because control case sessions, analytic sessions, don't necessarily comprise the dominant portion of our working weeks. And this may be a common experience. At the Columbia University Center for Psychoanalytic Training and Research, Cherry, Rosenberg, and Caligor (2018) developed a course for advanced candidates challenging them to integrate what they had learned about practicing psychoanalysis during training with their ongoing knowledge about psychotherapy practice. The idea followed the premise that in our current day and age psychoanalytically trained candidates report practicing psychodynamic psychotherapy, with patients visiting one or two times per week and sitting upright and facing the clinician, much more than they do formal psychoanalysis. Next, the authors asked candidates about how much analysis versus psychotherapy they expected to practice after graduation. Half expected their practices to be 25% psychoanalytic. A few others anticipated practicing "mostly" psychotherapy or else expecting a 50-50 split. We read these results soberly, feeling disappointed that analysis as a practice may be rare, though its ideas may be prospering. We think about our control cases, or the fewer patients who will accept invitations to the couch three or four times per week for an indeterminate spell. Will these patients consider how rare their commitment is, how precious it may be to them and to us?

In suggesting that analysis is common and that our experience practicing it is prodigious, our noses have grown, though maybe not so much from lying as from holding back, being careful, inhibited.

I wonder about hypocrisy within the inclusion/exclusion debate, for example. I wonder about the meaning of the numbers, that reduction in requirements, which implies that inclusion means making training easier, as in less time consuming, less expensive for the less resourced, the disadvantaged. This pertains to candidates but also our prospective patients. A man calls me up asking for my time. We met over a handful of sessions a few years ago—sessions he enjoyed. Says they were the best therapy sessions he ever had and he wants more of this in-depth therapy or analysis thing I do. Only he ghosted me—meaning, he disappeared, didn't show for subsequent sessions and didn't respond to outreach efforts. Then he called some months later, apologized for his previous disappearance, claimed he got caught up in "drama," was homeless, then incarcerated. Now he was back on his feet, wanting a second chance at that in-depth therapy that he appreciated. I gave him a second chance, as I have done with numerous patients who are like him, but he wasn't an analytic case, much less a control case. Also, I didn't get paid for his no-shows. The public funding source that reimburses his treatment does not pay for no-shows, nor does it reimburse multiple sessions per week unless deemed "medically necessary" due to an acuity of existing symptoms, not a desire for more understanding from a patient whose symptoms have abated and whose abatement may last *because* of that understanding. Furthermore, these patients do not incur a cost

for their absences, which is at once a reasonable if defeatist accommodation to their circumstances. This "institutional" policy does not seem to help incentivize treatment, and it's unofficially apparent that it generates more absences in treatment than private fee-paying arrangements.

There's a limit to how many low-fee, high-risk cases I can take on my practice caseload—how many hours I can devote to patients who cannot pay for a multiple-session commitment to psychoanalysis, week after week, possibly for years. Also, the lives of the disadvantaged are beset with numerous and varied obstacles that make difficult a regular commitment to mental health care. The man in my vignette resumed sessions for a spell, and again appeared to appreciate the insights that he received and, in some instances, generated himself. His external circumstances also seemed to stabilize for a while. Then he disappeared again, not showing for consecutive sessions, not returning calls, text messages. Meanwhile, I attempted to refer low-fee cases whom I did not have room in my schedule for to colleagues—typically other candidates, or extant community members from the institute. However, the would-be patients were failing to land with my colleagues, reporting that they could not negotiate an acceptable fee. All too many analytic colleagues were charging rates that were prohibitively expensive, and none were contracted with public funding sources that may have enabled treatment for these individuals, either for free or with a nominally low cost. I know that low-cost referral services exist, both within psychoanalytic circles and without, and I'm sure that many professionals do provide their fair share of low-fee services, even managing to provide a multiple-session-per-week arrangement for some who would not be included historically. At the same time, I wonder how many are paying lip service to this issue but only taking the cases that will meet control case requirements, suiting their needs and not those of individuals or communities. I have my analyst's voice in my head, saying, *You're focusing on numbers, the external.* It's a critique, though that's only how I'm taking it. Anyway, this is a token piece of resistance on my part, and otherwise my resistances to psychoanalysis are few and weak, and I'm done saying I'm done. Everything is all right. The struggle feels nearly over. I have won a victory over myself. I love psychoanalysis.

Maybe I'll wait for the finish line of graduation to say something like this, about the vulnerable, including myself. It'll be like a doorknob disclosure, something said on the way out, protesting but with less humor—avoiding but only a little. A touch of peekaboo on the way out. As for the institute, its requests for feedback will be less personal. Perhaps it will come as a text invite for a survey, with an attached link that reads, "Tell us how we did." Maybe the parting shots or musings will be something to say to colleagues as we reunite from time to time. Our cohort said it would get together postseminar, or postgraduation, perhaps at that bar that's kitty-corner to the San Francisco center. Venturing back there, I step across the class divide, enter the alley that leads to the center, the one shadowed by feral surroundings. I tread along the new macadam path that cuts through the garden that flanks the building. Inside, not much has changed, except that a spring cleaning has occurred. The long-mooted new HVAC system seems to be working well. The carpets have been cleaned. Outside, the sidewalk still reeks and the stains about the doorway are still there, but the interior has been sprayed for pests, of the noncandidate variety, of course.

As for the candidates, or my cohort at least, we said we'd hang out around here or nearby and decompress, share about the program experience, laugh, thumb our Pinocchio noses at or share endearments about its principals. We took our time, then seized upon a date finally. By the time we'd found time to meet together, a couple of us had reached the rainbow—that is, graduated—and seem relieved and rested. Together, we did what I expected we'd do: we got a few things off our chests, addressed a few grievances, including one or two that were between us. One exchange was a buzzed contretemps about how I'd once broken ranks and sided with the tribal enemy that is faculty. Otherwise, it was a party that didn't exactly last until dawn, but it recognized a camaraderie that was long unrealized. Maybe we need more time, more distance, to contemplate all of the questions that our training stoked. Perhaps we're like high school graduates whose received wisdom decrees that five-year intervals between meetings are called for. We'd need that time and space before talking about psychoanalysis and institutions again, to speak about what it all did to us, what we've done to ourselves. Maybe we'd say similar things in the future, riff off one another's thoughts. Or we'd deflect some more and speak of current events, institutional happenings.

Who will be the next president of the institute? Will long-overdue changes be made to curriculum? Will admission requirements be reviewed again and altered, having been voted on democratically? Will graduation requirements be further reduced, and will that manifest in greater inclusion of society's more vulnerable would-be psychoanalysts? Are we all back in our offices yet? Or have some of us resolved to never return to live interaction with patients? With all that covered, will conversation turn to life outside of psychoanalysis, like who is the next president of the nation? Reality, not fantasy. Once-autumn winds are now all-seasonal, blowing the fires up north but also in tropical climates, like Hawaii, and even in the Hollywood Hills. In the Southeast the wind is generally wetter, raising water levels above heads, battering coastlines. The innocent and not so innocent are suffering as we debate about neutrality and moral equivalence, some taking sides, some not. Are we taking a stand, as in posting our views on the ApsaA Listserve, dispensing wisdom, poems of lament when bad things happen? For those with fixed opinions about the doer/done-to equation, who think that facts define phenomena, psychoanalytic neutrality as a personal or collective identity will mean little. Candidates like myself will conjure graduation and beyond, thinking bad weather has little to do with psychoanalysis. Actually, it's not bad weather. It's something more.

I hallucinate elephants stomping through the center's mouthy auditorium and think of the words I'd say versus those I'd hold back. I'll pause, inject a silence, see how that feels, whether it's hostile or peaceful and inviting. I'll reflect that categorical imperatives are disappointing. That's all, maybe. There's more, always more, but the unfinished is mine. And I don't want to go into it if you want to know the truth.

Notes

Chapter 2

1 The period 2020 to 2023 surely spared numerous candidates, including myself, the kind of onerous movements I'm describing here. Phone or Zoom sessions and seminars rendered unnecessary much of the travel time that otherwise inflates a candidate's work and training schedule. I estimate that my work week was shortened by 10 hours per week, on average, by the COVID restrictions.

Chapter 5

1 At SFCP, current policy for full analytic training states that candidates must have three supervised control cases that meet three to five times per week and be in personal analysis with a training analyst three to five times per week. These requirements were passed by a ratification vote of analyst and candidate members in 2023.

References

Adler, A. (1917). *Study of organ inferiority and its psychical compensation* (S. E. Jellife, Trans.) Nervous and Mental Disease Publishing.

Bader, M. (1993). The analyst's use of humor. *Psychoanalytic Quarterly, 62*, 23–50.

Bergeret, J. (1973). Pour une métapsychologie de l'humour. *Revue Française de Psychanalyse, 37*(4), 539–565.

Bettelheim, B. (1982). *Freud and Man's Soul*. Vintage Books.

Bion, W. (1961). *Experiences in groups*. Tavistock.

Bion, W. (1967). Notes on memory and desire. *Psychoanalytic Forum, 2*, 272–273.

Brenner, C. (1981). Defense and defense mechanisms. *Psychoanalytic Quarterly, 50*, 557–569.

Chabert, C. (2007). La malaise dans la culture et la question du surmoi. *Canadian Journal of Psychoanalysis, 15*, 215–237.

Cherry, S., Rosenberg, M., & Caligor, E. (2018). Teaching psychotherapy to psychoanalytic candidates. *Journal of the American Psychoanalytic Association, 66*(6), 1051–1064.

Coimbra de Matos, A. (2011). O humor segundo a psicopatologia. In *Relação de qualidade: penso em ti* (pp. 239–254). Climepsi.

Coltart, N. (1987). Diagnosis and assessment for suitability for psycho-analytic psychotherapy. *British Journal of Psychotherapy, 4*(2), 127–134.

Danto, E. (2007). *Freud's free clinics: Psychoanalysis and social justice*. Columbia University Press.

Director, L. (2005). Encounters with omnipotence in the psychoanalysis of substance users. *Psychoanalytic Dialogues, 15*(4), 567–586.

Dodes, L. (2003). *The heart of addiction: A new approach to understanding and managing alcoholism and other addictive behaviors*. Quill.

Donnet, J.-L. (2005). Surmoi. In A. Mijolla, B. Golse, S. Mijolla-Mellor, & R. Perron (Eds.), *Dictionnaire international de la psychanalyse* (pp. 1754–1756). Hachette Littératures.

Ehrlich, L. T. (2019). Teleanalysis: Slippery slope or rich opportunity. *Journal of the American Psychoanalytic Association, 67*(2), 249–279.

Ellman, S. (1991). *Freud's technique papers: A contemporary perspective*. Jason Aronson.

Fonagy, P. (2008). A genuinely developmental theory of sexual enjoyment and its implications for the psychoanalytic technique. *Journal of the American Psychoanalytic Association, 1*, 11–36.

Freud, A. (1936). *The ego and the mechanisms of defense*. International Universities Press.

Freud, S. (1900). The interpretation of dreams. In J. Strachey (Ed.), *The standard edition of the complete psychological works of Sigmund Freud.* Hogarth Press.
Freud, S. (1905). Jokes and their relation to the unconscious. In J. Strachey (Ed.), *The standard edition of the complete psychological works of Sigmund Freud* (Vol. 8). Hogarth Press.
Freud, S. (1911). Formulations on the two principles of mental functioning. In J. Strachey (Ed.), *The standard edition of the complete psychological works of Sigmund Freud* (Vol. 12, pp. 213–226). Hogarth Press.
Freud, S. (1913). On beginning the treatment. In J. Strachey (Ed.), *The standard edition of the complete psychological works of Sigmund Freud* (Vol. 12, pp. 121–144). Hogarth Press.
Freud, S. (1914). Remembering, repeating, and working through. In J. Strachey (Ed.), *The standard edition of the complete psychological works of Sigmund Freud* (Vol. 12, pp. 145–156). Hogarth Press.
Freud, S. (1915). Observations on transference-love. In J. Strachey (Ed.), *The standard edition of the complete psychological works of Sigmund Freud* (Vol. 12, pp. 159–171). Hogarth Press.
Freud, S. (1917). Mourning and melancholia. In J. Strachey (Ed.), *The standard edition of the complete psychological works of Sigmund Freud* (Vol. 14, pp. 237–258). Hogarth Press.
Freud, S. (1920). Beyond the pleasure principle. In J. Strachey (Ed.), *The standard edition of the complete psychological works of Sigmund Freud* (Vol. 18, pp. 1–64). Hogarth Press.
Freud, S. (1921). Group psychology and the analysis of the ego. In J. Strachey (Ed.), *The standard edition of the complete psychological works of Sigmund Freud* (Vol. 18). Hogarth Press.
Freud, S. (1923). The ego and the id. In J. Strachey (Ed.), *The standard edition of the complete psychological works of Sigmund Freud* (Vol. 19). Hogarth Press.
Freud, S. (1926). The question of lay analysis. In J. Strachey (Ed.), *The standard edition of the complete psychological works of Sigmund Freud* (Vol. 20). Hogarth Press.
Freud, S. (1994). L'humour. In J. Laplanche (Series Ed.), Bourguignon & Cotet (Vol. Eds.), *Ouvres completes: Vol. XVIII, 1926–1930* (pp. 135–140) (R. Lainé & J. Stute-Cadiot, Trans.). Presses Universitaires de France. (Original work published in 1927.)
Gabbard, G. (2020). The analyst and the virus. *Journal of the American Psychoanalytic Association, 68*(6), 1089–1099.
Gabbard, G., & Ogden, T. (2009). On becoming a psychoanalyst. *International Journal of Psychoanalysis, 90*, 311–327.
Gay, P. (1988). *Freud: A life for our time*. W. W. Norton.
Giovacchini, P. L. (1969). The influence of interpretation upon schizophrenic patients. *International Journal of Psychoanalysis, 50*, 179–186.
Giovacchini, P. L. (1972). Interpretation and the definition of the analytic setting. In P. L. Giovacchini (Ed.), *Tactics and techniques in psychoanalytic therapy* (Vol. 2, pp. 5–94). Jason Aronson.
Grossman, L. (2022). *The psychoanalytic encounter and the misuse of theory*. Routledge.
Grotstein, J. S. (1999). Humor and its relation to the unconscious. In J. Barron (Ed.), *Humor and psyche: Psychoanalytic perspectives* (pp. 69–86). Analytic Press.

Horney, K. (1924). On the genesis of the castration complex in women. *International Journal of Psychoanalysis, 5*, 50–65.
Horney, K. (1926). The flight from womanhood: The masculinity complex in women, as viewed by men and women. *International Journal of Psychoanalysis, 7*, 324–339.
Kanzer, M. (1980). Freud's "human influence" on the Rat Man. In M. Kanzer and J. Glenn (Eds.), *Freud and his patients* (pp. 232–239). Jason Aronson.
Klein, M. (1935). A contribution to the psychogenesis of manic-depressive states. In *Contributions to psychoanalysis, 1921–1945* (pp. 254–256). McGraw-Hill. (Original work published in 1931.)
Klein, M. (1946). Notes of some schizoid mechanisms. *International Journal of Psychoanalysis, 27*, 99–110.
Klein, M. (1957). *Envy and gratitude.* Hogarth Press.
Kohut, H. (1966). *Análise do self*. Imago Editora.
Kohut, H. (1971). *The analysis of the self: A systematic approach to the psychoanalytic treatment of narcissistic personality disorders*. International University Press.
Kohut, H. (1977). *The restoration of the self*. International University Press.
Kravis, N. (2017). The googled and googling analyst. *Journal of the American Psychoanalytic Association, 65*(5), 799–818.
Lansky, M. (2004). Conscience and the project of a psychoanalytic science of human nature: Clarification of the usefulness of the superego concept. *Psychoanalytic Inquiry, 24*(2), 151–174.
Laplanche, J., & Pontalis, J.-B. (1967). *Vocabulaire de la psychanalyse*. Presses Universitaires de France.
Ledoux, J. E. (1996). *The emotional brain: The mysterious underpinnings of emotional life*. Simon & Schuster.
Loewald, H. (1960). On the therapeutic action of psychoanalysis. *International Journal of Psychoanalysis, 41*, 16–33.
Mahony, P. J. (1986). *Freud and the Rat Man*. Yale University Press.
Makari, G. (2008). *Revolution in mind*. Harper/Perennial.
Maroda, K. (2022). *The analyst's vulnerability: Impact on theory and practice*. Routledge.
Masterson, J. (1976). *Psychotherapy of the borderline adult: A developmental approach.* Brunner/Mazel.
Masterson, J. (1981). *The narcissistic and borderline disorders: An integrated developmental approach.* Brunner/Mazel.
Meltzer, D. (1978). *The Kleinian development*. Karnac.
Meltzer, D. (1992). The claustrum and adolescence. In M. Harris Williams (Ed.), *Adolescence: Talks and papers by Donald Meltzer and Martha Harris* (pp. 199–203). Karnac Books.
Newirth, J. (2006). Jokes and their relation to the unconscious: Humor as a fundamental emotional experience. *Psychoanalytic Dialogues, 16*(5), 557–571.
Philips, A. (1995). *Terrors and experts*. Harvard University Press.
Philips, A. (2024). *On giving up.* Farrar, Straus & Giroux.
Pinheiro, M. T. C. (2011). *Um estudo exploratório sobre o sentido de humor e as suas relações com a culpa, a vergonha e a depressão* [master's thesis]. Universidade de Lisboa.
Reik, T. (1948). *Listening with the third ear: The inner experience of a psychoanalyst*. Grove Press.

Renik, O. (1994). Publication of clinical facts. *International Journal of Psychoanalysis, 75*, 1245–1250.
Rizzolatti, G., Fadiga, L., Gallese, V., & Fogassi, L. (1996). Premotor cortex and the recognition of motor actions. *Cognitive Brain Research, 3*, 131–141.
Russo, J. P. (2005). *The future without a past: The humanities in a technological society*. University of Missouri Press.
Schore, A. N. (2011). The right brain implicit self lies at the core of psychoanalysis. *Psychoanalytic Dialogues, 21*, 75–100.
Stoller, R. J. (1988). Patients' response to their own case reports. *Journal of the American Psychoanalytic Association, 36*, 371–391.
Tower, L. E. (1956). Countertransference. *Journal of the American Psychoanalytic Association, 4*, 224–265.
Tuckett, D. (2005). Does anything go? Towards a framework for the more transparent assessment of psychoanalytic competence. *International Journal of Psychoanalysis, 86*, 31–49.
Tuckett, D., Junkers, G., & Zachrisson, A. (2008). To be or not to be a psychoanalyst. *Psychoanalytic Inquiry, 28*, 288–308.
Wilson, M. (2003). The analyst's desire and the problem of narcissistic resistances. *Journal of the American Psychoanalytic Association, 51*, 71–99.
Winnicott, D. W. (1951). Transitional objects and transitional phenomena. In *Collected papers: Through pediatrics to psycho-analysis* (pp. 229–242). Hogarth Press.
Winnicott, D. W. (1958). The capacity to be alone. *International Journal of Psychoanalysis, 39*, 416–420.
Winnicott, D. W. (1974). Fear of breakdown. *International Review of Psychoanalysis, 1*, 103–107.
Winnicott, D. W. (1975). Hate in the countertransference (1947). In *Through paediatrics to psychoanalysis* (pp. 194–203). Basic Books.

Index

About the Author

Graeme Daniels, MFT, has been a practicing psychotherapist since 1996, working with individuals, couples, and groups and treating a variety of mental health conditions, in hospital and private practice settings. Since 2011, he has been a prolific author, writing and self-publishing several novels as well as three nonfiction works, the last of which, *Getting Real About Sex Addiction: A Psychodynamic Approach to Treatment*, coauthored with Joe Farley, MFT, was published by Rowman & Littlefield in 2022. In 2016, he published an 8,000-word academic article about object relations theory and the rock opera *Tommy* in the *Journal of Culture and Psychology*. He has made live professional presentations at the 2015 Society for the Advancement of Sexual Health (SASH) conference in San Diego, plus an online SASH conference in 2023, and at the 2017 and 2021 "Creativity and Madness" conferences in Santa Fe. These presentations drew sizable audiences for the presentations "The Psychology of *Tommy*" in 2017 and "Dr. Strangelove in the 21st Century, or How I Learned to Stop Worrying and Love the Virus" in 2021. Concurrently, he has provided annual training at San Francisco Bay Area mental health agencies on the Disorder of Self model of Dr. James Masterson, is a former faculty member at the West Coast Masterson Institute, and is a current instructor in the East Bay Year Long satellite program of the San Francisco Center for Psychoanalysis (SFCP). Graeme is also a postseminar analytic training candidate at SFCP. One other thing: Graeme is also a psychoanalyst.

www.ingramcontent.com/pod-product-compliance
Ingram Content Group UK Ltd.
Pitfield, Milton Keynes, MK11 3LW, UK
UKHW020208290926
15470UKWH00001B/57

9 798881 806408